C000139308

French

FOR COMMON ENTRANCE

13+

Revision Guide

James Savile

GALORE PARK
AN HACHETTE UK COMPANY

About the author

James Savile has taught French for over 20 years. He trained as an Independent Schools Inspector, has set French examinations for the Independent Schools Examinations Board and now works for them on various committees. James has been Head of Modern Languages in several prep schools and has been a Prep School Head for a number of years.

The Publishers would like to thank the following for permission to reproduce copyright material.

Acknowledgements

The author would like to thank Mr Hugh Walkington for his help with this book.

Every effort has been made to trace all copyright holders, but if any have been inadvertently overlooked, the Publishers will be pleased to make the necessary arrangements at the first opportunity.

Although every effort has been made to ensure that website addresses are correct at time of going to press, Galore Park cannot be held responsible for the content of any website mentioned in this book. It is sometimes possible to find a relocated web page by typing in the address of the home page for a website in the URL window of your browser.

Hachette UK's policy is to use papers that are natural, renewable and recyclable products and made from wood grown in sustainable forests. The logging and manufacturing processes are expected to conform to the environmental regulations of the country of origin.

Orders: please contact Bookpoint Ltd, 130 Milton Park, Abingdon, Oxon OX14 4SB.
Telephone: (44) 01235 827720. Fax: (44) 01235 400454. Email education@bookpoint.co.uk
Lines are open from 9 a.m. to 5 p.m., Monday to Saturday, with a 24-hour message answering service.
Visit our website at www.galorepark.co.uk for details of other revision guides for Common Entrance, examination papers and Galore Park publications.

ISBN: 978 1 5104 3501 8

First published in 2019 by

Hodder and Stoughton Ltd,

An Hachette UK Company

Carmelite House

50 Victoria Embankment

London EC4Y 0DZ

www.galorepark.co.uk

Impression number 4 3 2

Year 2023 2022 2021 2020

Illustrations by Aptara, Inc.

Typeset in India

Printed in Spain

A catalogue record for this title is available from the British Library.

FSC www.fsc.org
MIX
Paper from responsible sources
FSC™ C104740

Photo credits

p33 © Monkey Business/Fotolia.com; **p34** © Ivonne Wierink/Fotolia.com; **p44** (top) © jahmaica/123RF.com, (second row left) © Africa Studio/Shutterstock.com, (second row centre) © Jacob Wackerhausen/istockphoto, (second row right) © Kieren Welch/Fotolia.com, (third row left) © Den Rozhnovsky/Shutterstock.com (third row centre) © slp_london/Fotolia.com, (third row right) © donaveh/123RF.com, (bottom left) © De Visu/Fotolia.com, (bottom centre) © Natthawon Chaosakun /Shutterstock.com; **p51** (top left) © auremar/Fotolia.com, (top centre) © Fernando Sanchez Cortes/Shutterstock.com, (top right) © Orhan Çam/Fotolia.com, (bottom left) © CandyBox Images/Fotolia.com, (bottom centre) © goodluz/Fotolia.com, (bottom right) © Raisa Kanareva/Fotolia.com; **p53** (top) © pornchai7/Fotolia.com, (second row left) © Benjamin Simeneta/stock.adobe.com, (second row centre) © Mellimage/Fotolia.com, (second row right) © jurij_kachkovskij/123RF.com, (third row left) © dashingstock/Shutterstock.com, (third row centre) © ivonnewierink/123RF.com, (third row right) © studiophotopro/Fotolia.com, (bottom left) © veryolive/Fotolia.com, (bottom centre) © Witchcraft/Fotolia.com, (bottom right) © dule964/stock.adobe.com; **p54** (top) © wavebreakmediamicro/123RF.com, (middle) © Eléonore H/Fotolia.com, (bottom) © Getty Images/iStockphoto/Thinkstock/Eric Isselée; **p64** (top) © DONOT6_STUDIO/Shutterstock.com, (second row left) © Kybele - Fotolia.com, (second row centre) © Piotr AdamowiczFotolia.com (second row right) © Dima Moroz/Shutterstock.com, (third row left) © nexus 7/Shutterstock.com, (third row centre) © Photographee.eu/Shutterstock.com, (third row right) © Yantra/Fotolia.com, (fourth row left) © Elena Elisseeva/Fotolia.com, (fourth row centre) © lukeruk/Shutterstock.com, (fourth row right) © klikk/Fotolia.com, (bottom left) © mubus/Fotolia.com, (bottom right) © littleny/Fotolia.com; **p72** (top) © Shutterstock/alexandre zveiger, (second row left) © hazel proudlove/Fotolia.com, (second row centre) © Fotolia.com, (second row right) © non c/Shutterstock.com, (third row left) © 1000 words/Shutterstock.com, (third row centre) © Picture-Factory/Fotolia.com, (third row right) © yanlev/Fotolia.com, (bottom left) © bitterfly/iStock/Thinkstock, (bottom centre) © Monkey Business/Fotolia.com, (bottom right) © Wavebreak Media Ltd/123RF.com; **p82** (top left) © Evgeny Karandaev/Shutterstock.com, (top centre) © imstock/Fotolia.com, (top right) © bitt24/Shutterstock.com, (bottom left) © utima/123RF.com, (bottom centre) © Paul Maguire/Fotolia.com, (bottom right) © imagedb.com/Fotolia.com; **p84** (top) © Inna Zakharchenko/Shutterstock.com, (second row left) © Kostia Lomzov/Fotolia.com, (second row centre) © movingmoment/123RF.com, (second row right) © diamant24/Shutterstock.com, (third row left) © Nikolai Sorokin/Fotolia.com, (third row centre) © si evans/Fotolia.com, (third row right) © Liaurinko/Fotolia.com, (bottom left) © SGM/Shutterstock.com, (bottom centre) © Stockbyte/Getty Images Ltd/Fast Food SD175, (bottom right) © anskuw/123RF.com; **p85** (top left) © Mariusz Prusaczyk/Fotolia.com, (top right) © den-belitsky/stock.adobe.com, (bottom) © Pablo Scapincahis/Fotolia.com; **p86** (top left) © Delpixel/Shutterstock.com, (top centre) © Justin Kase RF/Alamy Stock Photo, (top right) © redzen2/Shutterstock.com, (second row left) © Baloncici/Shutterstock.com, (second row centre) © Alain Machet/Alamy Stock Photo, (second row right) © robert paul van beets/Shutterstock.com, (third row left) © karen roach/Shutterstock.com, (third row centre) © David Franklin/Shutterstock.com, (third row right) © Ed Buziak/Alamy Stock Photo, (fourth row left) © Francois Poirier/Shutterstock.com, (fourth row centre) © David Burton/Alamy Stock Photo, (fourth row right) © Chris Craggs/Alamy Stock Photo, (bottom left) © Tony Kwan/ Alamy Stock Photo, (bottom centre) © Kumar Sriskandan/Alamy Stock Photo, (bottom right) © Thomas Dekiere/Shutterstock.com; **p94** (top) © Jacek Chabraszewski/Fotolia.com, (second row left) © Africa Studio/Fotolia.com, (second row centre) © Alan Crawford/istockphoto.com, (second row right) © picsfive/Fotolia.com, (third row left) © LuckyImages/Shutterstock.com, (third row centre) © artproem/Shutterstock.com, (third row right) © Brent Hofacker/Shutterstock.com, (bottom left) © EQRoy/Shutterstock.com, (bottom centre) © berc/Fotolia.com, (bottom right) © Vladislav Gajic/Alamy Stock Photo; **p95** (top) © Mr Twister/Fotolia.com, (middle left) © Imagestate Media (John Foxx)/Natural Faces and Expressions SS76, (middle centre) © George Dolgikh/Fotolia.com, (middle right) © Smileus/Fotolia.com, (bottom left) © Serhiy Kobyakov/Fotolia.com, (bottom right) © Anton Starikov/Shutterstock.com; **p96** (top) © klikk/Fotolia.com, (second row left) © Anton Starikov/Shutterstock.com, (second row centre) © Ingram Publishing Limited/Ingram Image Library 500-Sport, (second row right) © ESLINE/Fotolia.com, (third row left) © Jacek Chabraszewski/Fotolia.com, (third row centre) © Smileus/Fotolia.com, (third row right) © Nolte Lourens/Fotolia.com, (bottom left) © nickolae/Fotolia.com, (bottom centre) © Misha/Fotolia.com, (bottom right) © Ingram Publishing Limited/Ingram Image Library 500-Education; **p97** (left) © Michael Pettigrew/Fotolia.com, (centre) © Mr Twister/Fotolia.com, (right) © Diego Cervo/Shutterstock.com; **p104** (top left) © Monkey Business Images/Shutterstock.com, (top centre) © Nikola Bilic, (top right) © gani_dteurope/Fotolia.com, (middle left) © S.Borisov/Shutterstock.com, (middle centre) © Monkey Business/Fotolia.com, (middle right) © Nolte Lourens/Fotolia.com, (bottom left) © Zovteva/Shutterstock.com, (bottom centre) © Getty Images/iStockphoto/Thinkstock, (bottom right) © Anton Starikov/Shutterstock.com; **p105** (top left) © littleny/Fotolia.com, (top centre) © LuckyImages/Shutterstock.com, (top right) © Vladislav Gajic/Alamy Stock Photo, (middle left) © Mr Twister/Fotolia.com, (middle centre) © Diego Cervo/Shutterstock.com, (middle right) © Brand X/ Photolibrary Group Ltd/Teenage CD X182, (bottom left) © sondem/Shutterstock, (bottom centre) © Morrowind/Shutterstock.com, (bottom right) © Laurence Gough/Fotolia.com; **p107** (top) © Kent Weakley/iStockphoto.com, (second row left) © Lim Jerry/Fotolia.com, (second row centre) © Korelidou Mila/Shutterstock.com, (second row right) © Audrius Merfeldas/Shutterstock.com, (third row left) © Maksym Yemelyanov/Fotolia.com, (third row centre) © Bejim/Shutterstock.com, (third row right) © Margo Harrison/Shutterstock.com, (bottom left) © sp4764/Fotolia.com, (bottom centre) © tnehala/Fotolia.com, (bottom right) © Studio KIWI/Shutterstock.com; **p108** (left) © S.Borisov/Shutterstock.com, (right) © artproem/Shutterstock.com; **p115** (top) © sumroeng chinnapan/Shutterstock.com, (second row left) © rich/Fotolia.com, (second row centre) © Getty Images/Digital Vision/Thinkstock, (second row right) © Jim Lopes/Shutterstock.com, (third row left) © Imagestate Media (John Foxx)/Vol 13 Backgrounds & Structures, (third row centre) © Olesia Bilkei/123RF.COM, (third row right) (bottom left) © sytilin/Fotolia.com, (bottom centre) © villorejo/Shutterstock.com, (bottom right) © Christopher Bradshaw/Fotolia.com; **p122** (left) © Gorilla/Fotolia.com, (right) © Africa Studio/Fotolia.com; **p127** (top) © rangizzz/Shutterstock.com, (second row left) © Business stock/Shutterstock.com, (second row centre) © Samuel Borges Photography/Shutterstock.com, (second row right) © RusN/iStock/Thinkstock/Getty Images, (third row left) © diego cervo/Fotolia.com, (third row centre) © Piotr Marcinski/Fotolia.com, (third row right) © denisnata/123RF.com, (bottom left) © Kurhan/Fotolia.com, (bottom centre) © Valua Vitaly/Fotolia.com, (bottom right) © Nicholas Piccillo/Shutterstock.com; **p128** (top) © Michael Pettigrew/Fotolia.com, (bottom left) © Kurhan/Fotolia.com, (bottom right) © istockphoto.com/Alan Crawford

Contents

Introduction

About this book

This revision guide has been written for pupils studying French for the Independent Schools Examinations Board (ISEB) Common Entrance examination at both Level 1 and Level 2.

Later in this Introduction is a description of the four papers that make up the examination: Speaking, Listening, Reading and Writing, with each skill comprising 25% of the exam. Candidates will find it helpful to know the format of each paper and to familiarise themselves with the style of questions they will meet.

Chapter 1 covers all the grammar candidates need to know, and some practice exercises are provided to test their knowledge and understanding. This is followed by a useful chapter on how to approach the Writing paper, which is for many candidates the most challenging part of the examination.

Subsequent chapters cover all the Common Entrance topics (see under 'Topics' later in this Introduction for the list of CE topics), with sample CE-style questions giving candidates practice in the four skills. You will find lots of important vocabulary and useful phrases in each chapter to help you revise.

Free audio download

Parts of this book refer to related audio material. Wherever there is related audio material you will see this symbol:

The audio material is available as a free download on the Galore Park website. Go to www.galorepark.co.uk/frenchaudio to download the audio. You can match the track number in the symbol to the track number in the audio download.

Level 2

Level 2 in the syllabus

The latest ISEB syllabus for French describes two tiered papers: Level 1 and Level 2. This book includes information on the syllabus (see under 'Syllabus information' later in this Introduction) and highlights some content that is only applicable to Level 2 candidates with the symbol shown above, on the left. Please note there are two topics that are only required for Level 2 candidates: 'Understanding tourist information' and 'Pocket money'. Syllabus information and Level 1 specimen papers are available from the ISEB (www.iseb.co.uk).

Revision

As well as looking in detail at the four skills of Speaking, Listening, Reading and Writing, it is important to think about your revision in general.

Get the best out of your brain

- Give your brain plenty of oxygen by exercising. You can revise effectively if you feel fit and well.
- Eat healthy food while you are revising. Your brain works better when you give it good fuel.
- Think positively. Give your brain positive messages so that it will want to study.

- Keep calm. If your brain is stressed, it will not operate effectively.
- Take regular breaks during your study time.
- Get enough sleep. Your brain will carry on sorting out what you have revised while you sleep.

Get the most from your revision

- Do not work for hours without a break. Revise for 20–30 minutes then take a 5-minute break.
- Do good things in your breaks: listen to your favourite music, eat healthy food, drink some water, do some exercise and juggle. Do not read a book, watch TV or play on the computer; it will conflict with what your brain is trying to learn.
- When you go back to your revision, review what you have just learnt.
- Regularly review the facts you have learnt.

Get motivated

- Set yourself some goals and promise yourself a treat when the exams are over.
- Make the most of all the expertise and talent available to you at school and at home. If you do not understand something, ask your teacher to explain.
- Get organised. Find a quiet place to revise and make sure you have all the equipment you need.
- Use year and weekly planners to help you organise your time so that you revise all subjects equally. (Planners are available for download from www.galorepark.co.uk.)
- Use topic and subject checklists to help you keep on top of what you are revising (available for download from www.galorepark.co.uk).

Know what to expect in the exam

- Use past papers to familiarise yourself with the format of the exam.
- Make sure you understand the language examiners use.

Before the exam

- Have all your equipment and pens ready the night before.
- Make sure you are at your best by getting a good night's sleep before the exam.
- Have a good breakfast in the morning.
- Take some water into the exam if you are allowed.
- Think positively and keep calm.

During the exam

- Have a watch on your desk. Work out how much time you need to allocate to each question and try to stick to it.
- Make sure you read and understand the instructions and rules on the front of the exam paper.

- Allow some time at the start to read and consider the questions carefully before writing anything.
- Read all the questions at least twice. Do not rush into answering before you have a chance to think about it.
- If a question is particularly hard, move on to the next one. Go back to it if you have time at the end.
- Leave yourself a little time at the end to check over your work.

Revision techniques

As you are having to cover a lot of vocabulary, here is a list of points to remember when revising:

- Use the LOOK–COVER–WRITE–CHECK technique.
- Always revise words from French into English then from English into French.
- Revise a few words at a time and in short regular intervals over a period of time.
- Start revising well in advance, not at the last minute before a test or examination.
- Connect a picture to a word in your mind to help you remember it.
- Ask someone to test you.
- Remember that, as well as spelling French words correctly, you need to use the proper accents where appropriate.

Syllabus information

The following information is a transcript of the latest ISEB French syllabus.

Introduction

The revised Common Entrance French syllabus for examination at 13+ and/ or Scholarship Level has been devised with reference to the statutory programmes of study for languages for Key Stage 2 and Key Stage 3 respectively of the National Curriculum (2013). In preparing pupils for Common Entrance and beyond, teachers should focus on broadening and strengthening their pupils' competence in listening, speaking, reading and writing, through knowledge and understanding of key grammar constructions and vocabulary.

There are tiered papers: Level 1 and Level 2. Level 1 is aimed at candidates who have studied French for between 30 and 40 hours, or who find the language very difficult. At Level 1, the past tenses are not required in any paper.

Aims

A course leading to this examination should:

(i) develop the skills which will enable candidates to understand the written and spoken language and use the language effectively for purposes of practical communication

(ii) give candidates opportunities to take part in a broad range of linguistic activities

(iii) provide a basis for continuing study of the language and encourage independent learning, including the use of dictionaries, glossaries and ICT

(iv) give candidates opportunities to work with authentic language materials

(v) encourage interest in the target countries

(vi) provide enjoyment and stimulation

(vii) encourage positive attitudes towards the use of foreign languages and towards speakers of foreign languages.

Assessment objectives

The examination will test candidates' ability to:

AO1 show an understanding of the spoken language dealing with a range of familiar topics, and identify and note main points and specific details, including opinions

AO2 take part in short conversations, giving and obtaining information and opinions

AO3 show an understanding of a number of printed items, ranging from short, simple phrases to longer, more complex texts and identify and note main points and specific details, including opinions

AO4 produce pieces of writing, ranging from short phrases to longer passages in which they seek and convey information and opinions.

Syllabus content

Introduction

(i) The examination is based on the topics set out below. An asterisk * denotes a topic which is not required for Level 1.

(ii) The grammar section lists all the material which candidates for the examination should cover.

Topics

- language of the classroom
- house, home, daily routine and chores
- life and work at school
- time, dates, numbers and prices
- personal description
- family, friends and pets
- meeting people
- free-time activities
- holiday activities
- visiting a café or restaurant
- simple health problems
- description of a town or region
- finding the way and using transport
- shopping (e.g. for food, clothes, presents)

- weather
- pocket money*
- understanding tourist information*

Grammar

(i) An asterisk * shows grammar that is for recognition only/where appropriate to the candidate's ability/senior school requirements.

(ii) Note that Level 2 requires you to know all of Level 1 as well. If a grammar point is marked with an asterisk * in Level 1, you will need to be able to use this grammar (not just recognise it) in Level 2.

	Level 1	Level 2
verbs	present tense: (i) regular and common irregular (ii) common reflexive future tense with aller conditional: only je voudrais, j'aimerais *imperative forms infinitive after aller, aimer, détester, préférer, je voudrais *infinitive after vouloir, pouvoir, devoir interrogative using est-ce que	passé composé with avoir/être[1] *passé composé of reflexives imperfect (use of c'était and il y avait) *imperfect tense infinitive after il faut *interrogative using inversion [1] In order to access the top bands in the Speaking and Writing tests, candidates will be required to show ability to use the passé composé in open-ended tasks.
	negative expressions: ne … pas, *ne … jamais, *ne … rien idiomatic expressions: e.g. avoir chaud/froid/faim/soif/mal, faire + weather	ne … plus *ne … personne
nouns	genders and plurals of common nouns, including irregulars definite and indefinite article partitive article (and de/d' with quantity/negatives)	agreement of irregular adjectives superlatives demonstrative adjectives
adjectives	agreement and position of regular and irregular adjectives agreement of common irregular adjectives (e.g. blanc, beau, nouveau, vieux) possessives *comparatives	
adverbs	common adverbs *adverbs ending in -ment	
pronouns	subject personal pronouns, including on reflexive pronouns relative pronoun qui disjunctive pronouns: moi, toi	relative pronouns: qui and que/qu' direct and indirect object pronouns disjunctive pronouns
prepositions and conjunctions	common prepositions and conjunctions *depuis and present tense	
numerals	cardinal numbers: 0–1000 *ordinal numbers: 1–10 dates and time: 12-hour and 24-hour clock	

What is in the Common Entrance examination?

The Common Entrance examination is divided into four equal sections (each worth 25%): Speaking, Listening, Reading and Writing. Outlines of the details of each of these sections follow. Be aware that the final examinations for the Listening and Speaking sections are a few weeks earlier than the Reading and Writing sections. Your teacher will tell you when they are.

The Speaking paper

The Level 1 examination will consist of a discussion on two prepared topics, each lasting about two minutes. You will choose the topics yourself from this list:

- house, home, daily routine and chores
- free-time and holiday activities
- life and work at school
- personal description, family, friends and pets.

In each of the discussions, you will talk for about 30 seconds without being interrupted and your teacher will then ask you approximately three or four questions.

Each discussion will be marked out of 10, with marks being given for relevant communication, accuracy and quality of language. The total mark out of 20 will be scaled up to give a mark out of 25.

The Level 2 examination will consist of three sections:

- Level 2 a role play *(9 marks)*
- Level 2 a discussion on a topic that you have chosen and prepared *(8 marks)*
- Level 2 a discussion on a topic that your teacher chooses. *(8 marks)*

Level 2 Role play

Your teacher will give you a role play and you will be asked to carry out six tasks in French. The paper that your teacher gives you will have English instructions on it. Before the role play begins, you will have ten minutes' preparation time. You may use a bilingual dictionary during this time, but you may not make notes, nor may you take any written notes into the examination room.

You will not need the **passé composé**, the conditional or the imperfect tense in the role play, except perhaps for the phrases **je voudrais**, **c'était** and **il y avait.**

The role play will be from any area of the syllabus but, as you will see during practice sessions, there are some common phrases that may come up in any situation. If you learn these phrases before your examination, you should do well in the role play. Many pupils find this an easy way to pick up marks. A list of these phrases follows this section. Remember that you do not have to translate each task word for word. You can adapt the instruction to suit the phrases you know. For example, you might be asked to say: 'Would you like to go to the match with me?' You could simply say: **Tu veux aller au match avec moi?** This means: 'Do you want to go to the match with me?' It is not an exact translation of what you were asked to say, but the meaning is the same.

During the role play, your teacher will ask you, in French, a question that you have not prepared for, and you will need to answer it in French.

Remember that you only have to give a short answer, as long as it is appropriate. If one word is suitable, then that is fine.

A very important thing to think about in your role play is whether you have to use **tu** or **vous**. If your teacher is playing the part of a shopkeeper, teacher, waiter, etc., you must address them with **vous**. If they are playing the part of a friend, then you should use **tu**.

Look at the topic chapters (Chapters 3–9) in this book for examples of role plays.

Useful phrases for role plays

This is a list of some of the most common phrases (questions and answers) for many of the role plays. Others are included in the topic chapters. If you learn these, you will be well on your way to producing a high-quality role play.

Est-ce que ...?	*Turns any statement into a question*
Est-ce que je dois ...?	Must I ...?
Est-ce que tu aimes ...?	Do you like ...?
Est-ce que vous aimez ...?	Do you like ...?
Est-ce qu'il y a ...?	Is there ...?/Are there ...?
Est-ce qu'il faut ...?	Is it necessary to ...?
Est-ce que tu veux ...?	Do you want ...?
Est-ce que vous voulez ...?	Do you want ...?
Est-ce que je peux ...?	Can I ...?
Puis-je ...?	Can I ...?
Est-ce que tu peux ...?	Can you ...?
Est-ce que vous pouvez ...?	Can you ...?
Est-ce que tu as ...?	Do you have ...?
Est-ce que vous avez ...?	Do you have ...?
C'est ...?	Is it ...?
C'est combien?	How much is it?
Ça fait combien?	How much is it?
Qu'est-ce que c'est?	What is it?
À quelle heure ...?	At what time ...?
C'est loin d'ici?	Is it far from here?
C'est quelle direction?	Which direction is it?
Qu'est-ce que tu veux?	What do you want?
Combien de ...?	How many ...?
Quand ...?	When ...?
Où est ...?	Where is ...?
Où se trouve ...?	Where is ...?
Où sont ...?	Where are ...?
Où se trouvent ...?	Where are ...?
Il y a ...	There is .../There are ...
Je dois ...	I must/I have to ...
Je vais ...	I go/I am going ...
J'ai ...	I have ...
D'accord	OK

How is the role play marked?

Your teacher will mark the oral examination. Each of your responses in the role play will be awarded 0, ½ or 1 mark, up to a maximum of 6 marks.

0 Failure to communicate
½ The task is partly carried out; there may be considerable hesitation
1 Full communication (minor errors that do not affect communication will be allowed)

You will also be awarded a maximum of 3 marks for the quality of your language.

Level 2

A discussion on a topic that you have chosen

You can choose any topic from the list in Level 1 or a topic in connection with a country where the target language is spoken:

- a town or region
- a regional or national celebration
- an artist (painter, sculptor, writer, composer, etc.)
- a historical figure
- a sportsman/sportswoman.

The discussion will last for about two minutes. You will introduce your topic for about 30 seconds and your teacher will then ask you at least four questions during the rest of the two minutes. You should show use of the present tense, the **passé composé** and the near future.

The prepared topic will be marked out of 8. Credit will be given for relevant, spontaneous communication, appropriate response to the questions and the quality of the language used.

Tips for a quality discussion

- Once you have chosen your topic, talk to your teacher and involve him/her in the preparation.
- Make sure that the topic is not too obscure, as the vocabulary may be difficult.
- Make sure that your first sentence introduces the topic. A good way to start is to say:

Je vais vous parler de …	I am going to talk to you about …

- Think about the balance of detail so that the discussion is interesting and not tedious. Remember that it is your chance to show off!
- Avoid long lists of vocabulary as this will eat into your time.
- Try to use a range of tenses if you can.
- Practise your presentation and, if possible, record yourself so that you can hear how you come across.
- Do not rush, as this will sound unnatural. Speak at a normal pace, trying not to hesitate.
- When you practise, be aware of the timescale and try to time yourself if possible.
- Think about the types of questions your teacher might ask you and prepare suitable answers.

- Give your opinion whenever possible rather than just narrate. Use phrases such as:

Je crois que …	I think that …
À mon avis …	In my opinion …

- Remember that it is a conversation between you and the teacher but you should always do the majority of the talking.

Level 2

A discussion on a topic that your teacher chooses

You will have an unprepared discussion for about two minutes on any/all of the topics from the list in Level 1, but this will not overlap with the prepared topic. You should show a range of vocabulary and grammar, and use the present tense, the **passé composé** and the near future.

This discussion will be marked out of 8 in the same way as the prepared topic.

The Listening paper

The Listening paper will be based on a number of short passages recorded on a CD. Instructions will be given in English. There will be 25 questions, usually arranged in five sections.

Before the examination

Your teacher will prepare you for your examination and, in the process, give you practice exercises. This will help you tune your ear to listening to French. If you want further practice, ask your teacher for more examples that you can use in your free time. Your school may have a French **assistant(e)** who could help you; this can be very useful as it enables you to hear regional accents.

You may also be able to watch French television or listen to French radio, which you can also access on the internet. You would not be expected to understand it all but it can be good practice to listen out for key words. If you do this, ensure that you have no distractions and that you can concentrate.

You need to practise listening to French without seeing the person who is speaking. If you are listening to the television, turn away from the screen so that you cannot see the person. In lessons you may be allowed to listen to your teacher with your eyes closed for a while.

During the examination

When the examination starts, the voice on the CD will read out the instructions for you. Listen carefully and follow them on the front page of your exam paper, where you will find them written down.

You will be given time to read the questions at the start. In Common Entrance, this is two minutes. During this time you can do a lot of preparation. Make sure that you understand all of the questions and know exactly what is expected of you. In your preparation in class you should be made aware of what you have to do in each type of exercise.

While you and your fellow pupils may not be able to control noises from outside, you can ensure that you do not distract each other during the examination. For example, do not tap your pen lid on the desk and, if you know that you have a cold or a cough, take something to soothe your throat.

Even if you think you have answered the questions after listening only once, you must listen just as carefully the second time through as you may have made a mistake.

Remember that you can change your mind but you must make your final answer clear to the examiner. You can take notes at any time so it might be an idea, for example, if you hear a number or a date, to scribble down in French what you hear and work it out later.

All questions have an introduction, which explains in English what you have to do.

Types of questions

There will be a range of test-types in English: these might include multiple choice, true/false, table/grid completion, putting symbols on a map/plan, box-ticking, matching the recording with visual/verbal options, completing sentences/pictures, linking opinions with speakers, correcting a passage with mistakes highlighted, choosing correct answers or answering questions in English.

Three pictures to choose from

In this type of exercise you have to listen to what is said and decide which picture is most suitable.

- If it is a question about time, be sure to listen carefully to the numbers and the specific time phrases, such as 'half past' or 'minutes to'. If you hear the word **moins** it will mean 'minutes to'.
- If it is a question about clothes or appearance, listen carefully for words such as 'long' and 'short' or 'small' and 'big'.
- If it is a question about directions, listen carefully for words such as 'left' (**gauche**), 'right' (**droite**) or 'straight on' (**tout droit**). Make sure that you do not confuse 'right' and 'straight on'. Listen also for 'after' (**après**) and 'before' (**avant**).

Choosing a picture

In this type of question you have to listen to what is said and choose the correct picture. You have eight pictures to choose from and each one can only be used once. In the time before the start of the question, make sure that you are aware of what is in each picture.

Each picture will represent a mini topic such as a room in the house or an area of the school. Ask yourself what words may be used for each one. For example, if it is a picture of a bedroom you should be listening out for the usual words such as 'bed', 'wardrobe', 'table', etc. but also phrases such as 'getting dressed', 'going to bed' and other daily routines.

Multiple-choice phrases

In this type of question you have to choose one of the three or four possible answers. The possible answers in each question will have a common theme so think through the possible vocabulary while waiting for the CD. For example, the answers may be Friday, Saturday or Sunday so you need to think about the days of the week in French.

True or false

Read the questions and tick TRUE or FALSE. While waiting for the CD, think through the vocabulary that you might hear for each question. For example, if the question says 'The garden is big', think about words for size.

One-word answers

You may be asked to simply write one word. For example, if it is a spelling question in which you have to listen to people spell out certain words, listen carefully and then check your answer by asking yourself if it is a word that you know and if the spelling is correct.

Answering questions

If you have a question in English, you have to answer in English. As always, make sure that you read the instructions.

Gap-filling questions

In this type of question, you will be presented with a passage in which some words are missing. Below the passage will be a box containing a number of words. There are normally more words than you need, so do not panic! Look at the words in the box and work out what types of words they are.

They could be nouns, verbs, adjectives, adverbs, pronouns, prepositions, articles or conjunctions. In the case of nouns and adjectives, you will need to work out whether they are masculine or feminine and singular or plural. For the verbs, you will need to work out which part of the verb it is, which you can do by looking at the ending.

At the end of the examination

Always check your answers and make sure that you have written what you think you have written. If you have not been able to answer a question and have therefore left it blank, think about the context and possible answers. If you still are not able to answer the question, have a guess. Never leave a question unanswered as you will automatically receive zero for it. Every mark is 1% of your total. You have two minutes at the end of the Common Entrance examination to check through your answers.

The Reading paper

The Reading paper for Common Entrance is made up of 25 questions for Level 1 and Level 2, arranged in five sections.

Types of questions

Matching up pictures with phrases
In this type of exercise you need to read the sentence or sentences and decide which picture best matches what you have read. As in all sections, there will be an example on the examination paper.

Reading a passage and choosing one of several pictures
In this type of question you will be asked to read a passage and then some questions. For each question there will be several pictures and one of them will represent the answer. The questions will come in the order of the passage. Be sure to know your question words for this type of exercise. If you do not know which picture is correct, try to use a process of elimination. In other words, you may know that one of the pictures is definitely not correct, so you are then left with just two. Look at the detail in the pictures as this may help you. If you see a picture of a thin man wearing a shirt, trousers and shoes, think about the possible vocabulary that might appear in the passage.

True or false
In this type of question you will see a short passage. Read the text and indicate whether the statements are TRUE or FALSE by ticking the correct box. If you are not sure, make sure that you choose one of them as you have a 50–50 chance.

Connecting a phrase to part of a passage
This types of exercise can present itself in various forms. For example, you may be given a diary extract and have to say when things happened or you may have a few passages with people talking about themselves and then have to write the correct name next to each of a number of phrases.

Gap-filling questions
In this type of question you will be presented with a passage in which some words are missing. Below the passage will be a box in which there will be a number of words. There are normally more words than you need, so do not panic! Before reading the passage, look at the words in the box and work out what types of words they are. They could be nouns, verbs, adjectives, adverbs, pronouns, prepositions, articles or conjunctions. In the case of nouns and adjectives, you will need to work out whether they are masculine or feminine and singular or plural. For the verbs, you will need to work out which part

of the verb it is, which you can do by looking at the ending. Then read the passage and you should be able to work out what type of word would fit each blank.

Longer reading passages

Here are some tips for how you should approach a longer reading comprehension:

- Read the instructions carefully.
- Read through the questions before reading the passage as they will give you clues as to what the subject of the passage is.
- Read the passage and work out which paragraph each answer may be in. Remember that all questions should come in a consecutive order.
- Look out for any key words. If you have a question about a journey, ask yourself what types of words might be in the passage.
- Answer as many questions as you can.
- By answering some of the questions you should be able to narrow down where the other answers are in the passage.
- Apply grammatical rules to break down the passage or words. For example:
  - French words ending with **-té** often end in -ty in English.
  - French adverbs ending with **-ment** would have -ly at the end in English.
- In some sections you may not need to understand every word in order to answer a question. You may just be able to skim the text.
- Never leave any of the questions unanswered. If all else fails, make an intelligent guess. You get nothing for a blank!

The Writing paper

Chapter 2 provides more detailed information and advice on how to tackle the Level 1 and Level 2 Writing papers.

In the Level 1 paper there will be four sections.

- In Section 1 you will be asked to write six items of vocabulary on a specific topic.
- In Section 2 you will be asked to complete a grammar multiple-choice exercise.
- In Section 3 you will be asked to write short sentences about five pictures.
- In Section 4 you will be asked to write a few short sentences on a given topic from the syllabus.

How will these questions be marked?

- Section 1: 1 mark per correct item of vocabulary, up to a maximum of 5 marks (total 5 marks)
- Section 2: 1 mark per question (total 5 marks)
- Section 3: Up to 2 marks per sentence, awarded as appropriate (total 10 marks)
- Section 4: 1 mark per sentence, awarded as appropriate (total 5 marks)

In the Level 2 paper you will have to do two exercises, as detailed below.

Level 2

Section 1: Grammar (10 marks)

This exercise requires you to translate five sentences into French and is designed to assess your Level 2 grammar knowledge.

The sentences will be given in English and some French words will be provided to help you. Nouns and their gender will be given, verbs will be in the infinitive, and adjectives will be shown in their masculine singular form. The French verbs **avoir** and **être** will not be given. You will not need to use the **passé composé** or the imperfect.

Up to 2 marks will be given for each sentence, with a total of 10 marks available for the exercise.

Level 2

Section 2 (15 marks)

This exercise requires you to write an email of between 80 and 120 words based on some prompts. You will be given five bullet points in French and English, and you will need to write about at least four of them. You will need to show knowledge of the present tense, the past and the near future.

You will be assessed on the quality of your language and your ability to communicate the necessary information.

How will this question be marked?

This question is marked out of 15, according to the following descriptors.

Marks	Content and communication
5	Responds fully to the task and communicates with no ambiguity in a coherent and detailed way.
4	Communicates relevant information clearly and elaborates all points.
3	Reasonable communication, but either one point not covered or the general coverage of the points lacks detail.
2	Communication takes place, but with limited coverage of the required points and there may be instances of repeated or irrelevant material.
1	Partial communication and some attempt to respond to the task.
0	Communicates no relevant information.

Marks	Quality of language
9–10	A range of grammar, vocabulary, idiom and structures, used confidently and accurately to include accurate use of the **passé composé**, as well as of the present and near future tenses; fluent, controlled and varied; errors may exist, but only in the most ambitious language.
7–8	A good level of accuracy, fluency, range of vocabulary and grammar, including some successful attempt at using the **passé composé**.
5–6	Uses a range of straightforward structures and vocabulary, which may include different tenses; more right than wrong; reasonably coherent and accurate.
3–4	Some awareness of verbs, but inconsistent overall; some range and variety of idiom, vocabulary and structures, but generally a weakness in application and accuracy.
1–2	Inaccurate, very simple sentence structure and very poor range of vocabulary; much repetition; limited knowledge of the language; only a few phrases or short sentences accurate enough to be recognisable.
0	Nothing coherent or accurate enough to be comprehensible.

1 Grammar section

This chapter sets out all the essential grammar that is required for Common Entrance (a copy of the syllabus is included in the Introduction, under 'Syllabus information'). If you have a solid grasp of the grammar, you will be able to speak and write accurate French, which is the key to success in your exam. Remember that every sentence has a verb, so it is particularly important to check carefully that you have put each one in the correct tense with the right ending. Learn your grammar and do not be shy of showing off your knowledge when you speak and write French.

1.1 Verbs

Glossary of terms:

Verb A verb is often called a 'doing word'.

Infinitive The infinitive of a verb is the 'to ...' form in English, e.g. 'to do'. In a dictionary or word list, French verbs are given in the infinitive form, e.g. **jouer** means 'to play'.

Tense The tense of the verb tells you when something happens, e.g. past, present, future.

Every verb table in French is always written in the following order:

Singular	
je	I
tu	you*
il	he, it (m.)
elle	she, it (f.)
Plural	
nous	we
vous	you* (plural, or formal singular and plural)
ils	they (m. or mixed group)
elles	they (f.)

*In French there are two words for 'you': **tu** and **vous**. **Tu** is used when addressing one (singular) person who is a member of your family or a friend, or when talking to an animal; **vous** is used if you are addressing an adult whom you do not know well (for example when talking to a shop assistant), or if addressing more than one person or animal (plural).

Verbs in French are either regular or irregular. Regular verbs are divided into three groups: **-er** verbs, **-ir** verbs and **-re** verbs.

The present tense of regular verbs

Note the three ways of translating the French present tense:

je mange – I eat, I am eating, I do eat

-er verbs

These are called **-er** verbs because their *infinitive* ends with **-er**. To form the present tense of the verb you take off the **-er**. This leaves you with what is called the 'stem'. Onto this you add the correct ending for each person (**je**, **tu**, etc.).

je* regard**e**	I watch	nous regard**ons**	we watch
tu regard**es**	you watch	vous regard**ez**	you watch
il regard**e**	he watches	ils regard**ent**	they (m.) watch
elle regard**e**	she watches	elles regard**ent**	they (f.) watch
on** regard**e**	one watches		

*Note that je is written j' if the next word begins with a vowel or a silent h.

For example: j'aime, j'écoute, j'habite.

**Note that the word on means 'one', but it is often used instead of nous to translate 'we'. It always takes the same verb ending as il/elle.

For example: on aime l'école (we like school).

Some common -er verbs:

acheter*	to buy	fermer	to close
adorer	to love	habiter	to live
aimer	to like	manger†	to eat
chanter	to sing	marcher	to walk
danser	to dance	montrer	to show
détester	to hate	nager	to swim
donner	to give	porter	to wear
écouter	to listen (to)	préférer††	to prefer
entrer	to enter	regarder	to look at, to watch
espérer**	to hope	travailler	to work

*Beware of the accent in some parts: j'achète, tu achètes, il achète, elle achète, on achète, ils/elles achètent but nous achetons, vous achetez.

**Watch the accent: j'espère, tu espères, il espère, elle espère, on espère, ils/elles espèrent, but nous espérons, vous espérez.

†Note the nous form of this verb: nous mangeons. This is so that it is pronounced with a soft *g*, not like the *g* in 'mango'!

††Watch the accents: je préfère, tu préfères, il préfère, elle préfère, on préfère, but nous préférons, vous préférez.

Test yourself 1 ✓

Put the verb in the correct form of the present tense and then translate the sentence into English. Answers are given at the back of the book.

Example:

Je ______ dans ma chambre. (danser)

Je *danse* dans ma chambre.

I dance in my bedroom.

(a) J'______ jouer au squash. (aimer)

(b) Tu ______ le film ce soir? (regarder)

(c) Il ______ dans le jardin. (travailler)

(d) Elle ______ un sandwich au jambon. (manger)

(e) Nous ______ la robe rose. (préférer)

(f) Vous ______ la radio? (écouter)

(g) Ils ______ dans la salle de classe. (entrer)

(h) Elles ______ dans un appartement. (habiter)

-ir verbs

These are called -**ir** verbs because their *infinitive* ends with -**ir**. To form the verb you take off the -**ir**. This leaves you with the stem. Onto this you add the correct ending for each person. An example is **finir** (to finish).

je fin**is**	I finish	nous fin**issons**	we finish
tu fin**is**	you finish	vous fin**issez**	you finish
il fin**it**	he finishes	ils fin**issent**	they (m.) finish
elle fin**it**	she finishes	elles fin**issent**	they (f.) finish
on fin**it**	one finishes		

Some common -ir verbs:

choisir	to choose	polir	to polish
grossir	to put on weight	punir	to punish
maigrir	to lose weight	réussir	to succeed

Test yourself 2 ✓

Put the verb in the correct form of the present tense and then translate the sentence into English. Answers are given at the back of the book.

Example:

Je _____ une tarte dans la pâtisserie. (choisir)

Je *choisis* une tarte dans la pâtisserie.

I am choosing a tart in the cake shop.

(a) Je _____ une glace. (choisir)

(b) Tu _____ tes devoirs? (finir)

(c) Il _____ les élèves méchants. (punir)

(d) Elle _____ tout le temps. (réussir)

(e) Nous _____ (grossir)

(f) Vous _____? (maigrir)

(g) Ils _____ les exercices dans la salle de classe. (finir)

(h) Elles _____ de nouveaux vêtements. (choisir)

-re verbs

These are called **-re** verbs because their *infinitive* ends with **-re**. To form the verb you take off the **-re**. This leaves you with the stem. Onto this you add the correct ending for each person. An example is **vendre** (to sell).

je vend**s**	I sell	nous vend**ons**	we sell
tu vend**s**	you sell	vous vend**ez**	you sell
il vend	he sells	ils vend**ent**	they (m.) sell
elle vend	she sells	elles vend**ent**	they (f.) sell
on vend	one sells		

Notice two things here:

First, the 'he' and 'she' forms of the verb have no ending.

Second, the plural endings are the same as the plural endings of -er verbs.

Some common -re verbs:

attendre	to wait (for)	répondre	to reply
descendre	to go down, to get off	tondre	to mow
entendre	to hear		

Test yourself 3 ✓

Put the verb in the correct form of the present tense and then translate the sentence into English. Answers are given at the back of the book.

Example:

J'_____ le bus. (attendre)

J'*attends* le bus.

I am waiting for the bus.

(a) Je _____ la pelouse. (tondre)
(b) Tu _____ les enfants? (entendre)
(c) Il _____ l'escalier. (descendre)
(d) Elle _____ aux questions. (répondre)
(e) Nous _____ une réponse à notre message électronique. (attendre)
(f) Vous _____ des glaces? (vendre)
(g) Ils _____ des légumes au marché. (vendre)
(h) Elles _____ de l'autobus devant l'église. (descendre)

Reflexive verbs

A reflexive verb is used when something is happening to the subject. An example is **se laver** (to wash (oneself) or to have a wash).

je **me** lave	I wash myself	nous **nous** lavons	we wash ourselves
tu **te** laves	you wash yourself	vous **vous** lavez	you wash yourself/yourselves
il **se** lave	he washes himself	ils **se** lavent	they (m.) wash themselves
elle **se** lave	she washes herself	elles **se** lavent	they (f.) wash themselves

Some common reflexive verbs:

se réveiller	to wake up	s'amuser	to have fun
se lever*	to get up	se balader	to stroll
se laver	to have a wash	se casser (la jambe)	to break (one's leg)
se doucher	to have a shower	se demander	to wonder
se raser	to shave	se dépêcher	to hurry
se brosser les dents	to brush one's teeth	se disputer	to have an argument
se coiffer	to do one's hair	s'entendre avec	to get on with (people)
s'habiller	to get dressed	s'intéresser à	to be interested in
se promener*	to go for a walk	se reposer	to rest
se déshabiller	to get undressed	se sauver	to run away
se coucher	to go to bed	se trouver	to be (situated)

*Watch the accent in this verb! Je me lève, tu te lèves, il/elle/on se lève, ils/elles se lèvent, but nous nous levons, vous vous levez. Se promener follows the same pattern.

Note that me, te and se change to m', t', s' when followed by a vowel or a silent h.

For example: je m'habille, tu t'amuses, ils s'entendent.

Test yourself 4

Put the verb in the correct form of the present tense and then translate the sentence into English. Answers are given at the back of the book.

Example:

Je ____ à vingt-deux heures. (se coucher)

Je *me couche* à vingt-deux heures.

I go to bed at 10 p.m.

(a) Je ____ dans ma chambre. (s'habiller)

(b) Tu ____ à sept heures trente. (se lever)

(c) Il ____ devant un miroir. (se raser)

(d) Elle ____ les dents dans la salle de bains. (se brosser)

(e) Nous ____ très tôt chaque matin. (se réveiller)

(f) Vous ____ à quelle heure? (se réveiller)

(g) Ils ____ après le petit-déjeuner (se coiffer)

(h) Elles ____ à l'histoire. (s'intéresser)

The present tense of irregular verbs

Irregular verbs are verbs that do not follow the pattern of any of the regular verb groups. Here are the four most common ones.

avoir	**to have**	**être**	**to be**
j'ai	I have	je suis	I am
tu as	you have	tu es	you are
il a	he has	il est	he is
elle a	she has	elle est	she is
nous avons	we have	nous sommes	we are
vous avez	you have	vous êtes	you are
ils ont	they (m.) have	ils sont	they (m.) are
elles ont	they (f.) have	elles sont	they (f.) are
aller	**to go**	**faire**	**to do/make**
je vais	I go	je fais	I do
tu vas	you go	tu fais	you do
il va	he goes	il fait	he does
elle va	she goes	elle fait	she does
nous allons	we go	nous faisons	we do
vous allez	you go	vous faites	you do
ils vont	they (m.) go	ils font	they (m.) do
elles vont	they (f.) go	elles font	they (f.) do

Test yourself 5

Fill in the missing words from the verbs opposite, as in the example, and then translate the sentences into English. Answers are given at the back of the book.

Example:

Je _____ au cinéma. (aller)

Je *vais* au cinéma.

I go to the cinema.

(a) Elle _____ grande. (être)
(b) Nous _____ une petite maison. (avoir)
(c) Il _____ du ski. (faire)
(d) Nous _____ au supermarché. (aller)
(e) Ils _____ amusants. (être)
(f) Elles _____ les cheveux longs. (avoir)
(g) Tu _____ au théâtre. (aller)
(h) Vous _____ du vélo. (faire)
(i) Je _____ très contente. (être)
(j) J'_____ deux frères. (avoir)

Avoir expressions

The following phrases use **avoir** although in English we use the verb 'to be':

avoir faim	to be hungry	avoir peur (de)*	to be afraid (of)
avoir soif	to be thirsty	avoir raison	to be right
avoir chaud	to be hot	avoir tort	to be wrong
avoir froid	to be cold	avoir honte	to be ashamed
avoir sommeil	to be sleepy	avoir l'air	to seem
avoir lieu	to take place	avoir envie de*	to want very much
avoir besoin de*	to need		

*Note that **de** may change to **d'** if followed by a vowel or a silent **h**.

For example: **tu as besoin d'une règle** (you need a ruler).

Test yourself 6

Translate the following sentences into French. Answers are given at the back of the book.

Examples:

I am thirsty. *J'ai soif.*

We are hungry. *Nous avons faim.*

(a) She is wrong.
(b) Peter is afraid of cows.
(c) You (*singular*) are very hot.
(d) My mother is right.
(e) I need a pen.

The following common verbs are also irregular and need to be learnt:

boire (to drink)	**croire** (to believe)	**courir** (to run)
je bois	je crois	je cours
tu bois	tu crois	tu cours
il boit	il croit	il court
elle boit	elle croit	elle court
nous buvons	nous croyons	nous courons
vous buvez	vous croyez	vous courez
ils boivent	ils croient	ils courent
elles boivent	elles croient	elles courent
devoir (to have to)	**dire** (to say)	**écrire** (to write)
je dois	je dis	j'écris
tu dois	tu dis	tu écris
il doit	il dit	il écrit
elle doit	elle dit	elle écrit
nous devons	nous disons	nous écrivons
vous devez	vous dites	vous écrivez
ils doivent	ils disent	ils écrivent
elles doivent	elles disent	elles écrivent
mettre (to put (on))	**lire** (to read)	**pouvoir** (to be able)
je mets	je lis	je peux
tu mets	tu lis	tu peux
il met	il lit	il peut
elle met	elle lit	elle peut
nous mettons	nous lisons	nous pouvons
vous mettez	vous lisez	vous pouvez
ils mettent	ils lisent	ils peuvent
elles mettent	elles lisent	elles peuvent
prendre (to take)	**sortir** (to go out)	**venir** (to come)
je prends	je sors	je viens
tu prends	tu sors	tu viens
il prend	il sort	il vient
elle prend	elle sort	elle vient
nous prenons	nous sortons	nous venons
vous prenez	vous sortez	vous venez
ils prennent	ils sortent	ils viennent
elles prennent	elles sortent	elles viennent
voir (to see)	**vouloir** (to want)	**ouvrir** (to open)
je vois	je veux	j'ouvre
tu vois	tu veux	tu ouvres
il voit	il veut	il ouvre
elle voit	elle veut	elle ouvre
nous voyons	nous voulons	nous ouvrons
vous voyez	vous voulez	vous ouvrez
ils voient	ils veulent	ils ouvrent
elles voient	elles veulent	elles ouvrent

Remember that on takes the same ending as il and elle.

For example: on boit (one drinks, we drink), on peut (one can, we can).

dormir (to sleep)	**partir** (to leave)
je dors	je pars
tu dors	tu pars
il dort	il part
elle dort	elle part
nous dormons	nous partons
vous dormez	vous partez
ils dorment	ils partent
elles dorment	elles partent

Test yourself 7

Put the verb in the correct form of the present tense and then translate the sentence into English. Answers are given at the back of the book.

Example:

Je ____ mon déjeuner à la cantine. (prendre)

Je *prends* mon déjeuner à la cantine.

I have my lunch in the canteen.

(a) Je ____ très contente. (être)

(b) Tu ____ quel âge? (avoir)

(c) Il ____ une chemise bleue. (mettre)

(d) Elle ____ la porte. (ouvrir)

(e) Nous ____ une lettre à notre oncle. (écrire)

(f) Vous ____ quelque chose à boire? (vouloir)

(g) Ils ____ au cinéma ce soir. (aller)

(h) Elles ____ chez nous à dix-neuf heures. (venir)

Depuis

Depuis means 'since' and is used to describe how long you have been doing something.

Use the present tense (not the perfect as in English) + **depuis** + a time expression. For example:

J'apprends le français depuis deux ans.	I have been learning French for two years.
Je joue au golf depuis trois mois.	I have been playing golf for three months.

The infinitive

Using the infinitive

The infinitive is the part of the verb that means 'to do', for example 'to eat', 'to play', 'to leave', 'to buy'.

In French the infinitive usually ends in **-er**, **-ir**, **-re** or **-oir**, for example **jouer** (to play), **finir** (to finish), **vendre** (to sell), **boire** (to drink), **avoir** (to have).

The following verbs can all be followed by an infinitive, giving you hundreds of opportunities to write and speak good French:

aimer	to like to	**j'aime parler français**	I like to speak French
adorer	to love to	**il adore voyager**	he loves to travel
préférer	to prefer to	**nous préférons rester ici**	we prefer to stay here
vouloir	to want to	**tu veux partir?**	do you want to leave?
pouvoir	to be able to (can)	**on peut visiter le château**	one can visit the castle
devoir	to have to (must)	**je dois travailler**	I have to work

Note too that in English we say 'I do not like danc**ing**' and 'I hate work**ing**' but you use the infinitive in French.

For example: **je n'aime pas danser, je déteste travailler.**

Some other useful phrases that are followed by an infinitive are:

je voudrais	I would like	**je voudrais visiter le Canada**	I would like to visit Canada
il faut	it is necessary	**il faut téléphoner**	it is necessary to phone

Test yourself 8

Translate the following sentences into French. Answers are given at the back of the book.

(a) I want to go out.

(b) Do you (**tu**) like to play tennis?

(c) We (**nous**) can go to the cinema.

(d) I would like to live in France.

(e) I hate doing the shopping.

(f) She must stay at home.

The immediate future

The immediate future is made by using the present tense of the verb **aller** and an infinitive. For example: **je vais nager** (I am going to swim), **nous allons danser** (we are going to dance).

See earlier under 'The present tense of irregular verbs' if you are unsure of the verb **aller**.

Test yourself 9

Translate the following sentences into French. Answers are given at the back of the book.

Example:
I am going to draw.
Je vais dessiner.

(a) She is going to arrive this afternoon.
(b) They (*masculine*) are going to play on the computer.
(c) He is going to get dressed.
(d) We are going to choose a book.
(e) Are you (*singular*) going to return to France next year?
(f) You (*plural*) are going to sing this evening.
(g) Paul is going to dance with Anne.
(h) They (*feminine*) are going to play cards after lunch.

Other uses of the infinitive

Here are some other uses of the infinitive (which are not essential for Common Entrance).

Venir de + infinitive

Used in the present tense, **venir de** means 'to have just ...'.

Use the present tense of the verb **venir** + **de** + an infinitive, for example: **Je viens d'arriver** (I have just arrived), **nous venons de manger** (we have just eaten).

Être en train de + infinitive

Être en train de means 'to be in the process of ...', 'to be busy' (doing), 'to be in the middle of' (doing).

Use any tense of the verb **être** + **en train de** + an infinitive, for example:

Je suis en train d'écouter la radio.	I am (in the process of) listening to the radio.
J'étais en train de regarder la télévision.	I was (in the process of) watching TV.

Être sur le point de + infinitive

Être sur le point de means 'to be about to ...'.

Use any tense of the verb **être** + **sur le point de** + an infinitive, for example:

Anna est sur le point d'écrire une carte postale.
Anna is about to write a postcard.
J'étais sur le point de finir mes devoirs quand j'ai vu un autre exercice.
I was about to finish my homework when I saw another exercise.

The conditional

Knowledge of the conditional (translating 'would') is not essential for Common Entrance. However, the following phrases will be useful:

Je voudrais + infinitive	I would like ...
J'aimerais + infinitive	I would like ...
Je devrais + infinitive	I would have to .../I ought to .../I should ...

For example:

Je voudrais être médecin.	I would like to be a doctor.
Je devrais faire mes devoirs.	I ought to do my homework.

Test yourself 10

Translate the following sentences into French. Use the previous sections ('Other uses of the infinitive' and 'The conditional') for examples. Answers are given at the back of the book.

(a) I have just eaten.

(b) She has just finished.

(c) We are (in the process of) drinking.

(d) They (*feminine*) are (in the process of) choosing.

(e) Matthieu is about to write a letter.

(f) He is about to start the match.

(g) I would like to go to the cinema.

(h) You (*singular*) ought to eat a sandwich.

The imperative

It is not essential to learn this for Level 1 in Common Entrance but you should be able to recognise it. In Level 2 you will need to be able to use it.

The imperative is the 'command' form of the verb, for example 'Come!', 'Go!', 'Wait!'

When you use the imperative, you need to know whether the person or persons you are addressing require **tu** or **vous**.

The imperative is simply formed by using the **tu** or **vous** form of the present tense, without **tu** or **vous**, for example:

Finis! **Finissez!**	Finish!	**Viens!** **Venez!**	Come!	**Attends!** **Attendez!**	Wait!

However, **-er** verbs drop the **-s** of the **tu** form:

Mange! **Mangez!**	Eat!	**Commence!** **Commencez!**	Begin!

There is only one exception to the rule about forming imperatives: the verb **être** (to be), which changes to **sois** and **soyez**, for example:

Sois sage! **Soyez sages!**	Be good!

Level 2

The passé composé

Talking in French about what has happened in the past is quite straightforward, provided you follow some simple rules.

You need the **passé composé** to say what you *did* or what you *have done*, for example 'I ate', 'I have eaten'.

The **passé composé** is so called because it is composed of two parts: part of **avoir** or **être** (this is called the auxiliary) and a past participle, for example:

Avons is the auxiliary and **regardé** is the past participle.

nous avons regardé	we watched

Suis is the auxiliary and **arrivé** is the past participle.

je suis arrivé	I arrived

You will learn in this chapter how to form the past participle of verbs and how to know whether the verb takes **avoir** or **être**.

Verbs using avoir as an auxiliary

For most verbs the auxiliary is the appropriate part of the present tense of the verb **avoir**. To this you add a past participle:

- To form the past participle for **-er** verbs, change the **-er** of the infinitive to **-é**.
- To form the past participle for **-ir** verbs, change the **-ir** of the infinitive to **-i**.
- To form the past participle for **-re** verbs, change the **-re** of the infinitive to **-u**.

Note that the auxiliary changes but the past participle does not change.

For example:
j'ai mangé, elle a mangé, il a fini, nous avons fini.

Test yourself 11

Change the verbs from the present tense to the **passé composé** and translate your answer into English. Answers are given at the back of the book.

Example:

Je range ma chambre.

J'ai rangé ma chambre.

I tidied my room.

(a) *Je finis* mes devoirs.

(b) *J'attends* l'autobus.

(c) *Il joue* aux cartes.

(d) *Elle choisit* de nouvelles chaussures.

(e) *Nous regardons* la télé.

(f) *Vous entendez* le bruit.

(g) *Ils répondent* aux questions.

(h) *Elles écoutent* de la musique.

Verbs that have irregular past participles

The following verbs use **avoir** as their auxiliary but their past participles are irregular, for example **j'ai bu, tu as dû, nous avons fait:**

Infinitive	Passé composé	English
avoir	j'ai eu	I had/I have had
boire	j'ai bu	I drank
conduire	j'ai conduit	I drove
connaître	j'ai connu	I knew (a person)
courir	j'ai couru	I ran
croire	j'ai cru	I believed
devoir	j'ai dû	I had to
dire	j'ai dit	I said
écrire	j'ai écrit	I wrote
être	j'ai été	I was/I have been
faire	j'ai fait	I did, I made
lire	j'ai lu	I read
mettre	j'ai mis	I put (on)
ouvrir	j'ai ouvert	I opened
pouvoir	j'ai pu	I was able (to)
prendre	j'ai pris	I took
recevoir	j'ai reçu	I received
rire	j'ai ri	I laughed
savoir	j'ai su	I knew
suivre	j'ai suivi	I followed
voir	j'ai vu	I saw
vouloir	j'ai voulu	I wanted

Note that we have given the English meanings as 'I drank', 'I saw', etc. but all these verbs can also be translated by 'I have drunk', 'I have seen', etc.

Test yourself 12 ✓

Translate the following sentences into French. Answers are given at the back of the book.

Example:

I opened the door.

J'ai ouvert la porte.

(a) I drank some lemonade.

(b) She drove the car.

(c) He did his homework.

(d) You (*singular*) wrote a letter.

(e) You (*plural*) have read a magazine.

(f) We ran very fast.

(g) They (*masculine*) put the clothes in their bedroom.

(h) They (*feminine*) had an accident.

Verbs using être as an auxiliary

The following verbs use **être** as their auxiliary:

Infinitive	Passé composé	English
aller	je suis allé	I went
arriver	je suis arrivé	I arrived
descendre	je suis descendu	I went down
devenir	je suis devenu	I became
entrer	je suis entré	I entered, I went in
monter	je suis monté	I went up
mourir	il est mort	he died
naître	je suis né	I was born
partir	je suis parti	I left
rentrer	je suis rentré	I went home
rester	je suis resté	I stayed
retourner	je suis retourné	I returned
revenir	je suis revenu	I came back
sortir	je suis sorti	I went out
tomber	je suis tombé	I fell
venir	je suis venu	I came

Mr Tramp's Red Van

'Mr Tramp's Red Van' is a good mnemonic for remembering most of the verbs that take **être**:

monter **rester** **tomber** **retourner** **aller** **mourir**
partir **sortir** **rentrer** **entrer** **descendre** **venir**
arriver **naître**

An important thing to remember when you use the verbs that take **être** is that the past participle is treated like an adjective and has to 'agree' with the noun or pronoun, for example: **la fille est allée, nous sommes partis, elles sont sorties.**

Test yourself 13

Translate the following sentences into French. Answers are given at the back of the book.

Example:

I was born in 2001.

Je suis né(e) en 2001.

In this answer, boys would say Je suis né but girls would add the extra -e and say Je suis née. The brackets are only there to show that the -e might be needed.

(a) I left at three o'clock.

(b) She went out at quarter past six.

(c) He arrived at the hospital with his parents.

(d) We went down to the kitchen.

(e) Did you (*plural*) go to the cinema yesterday evening?

(f) They (*masculine*) came to the café with their friends.

(g) They (*feminine*) entered the sitting room.

(h) You (*singular*) returned home at ten to four.

Test yourself 14

Use the chart that follows to write the phrases below in French. Answers are given at the back of the book.

(a) We finished.

(b) She left.

(c) We came.

(d) She played.

(e) The boys fell.

This chart should help you work out how to select the correct form of verbs in the **passé composé.** It may be useful to check that you know all the parts of **avoir** and **être** (provided earlier in the book, under 'The present tense of irregular verbs').

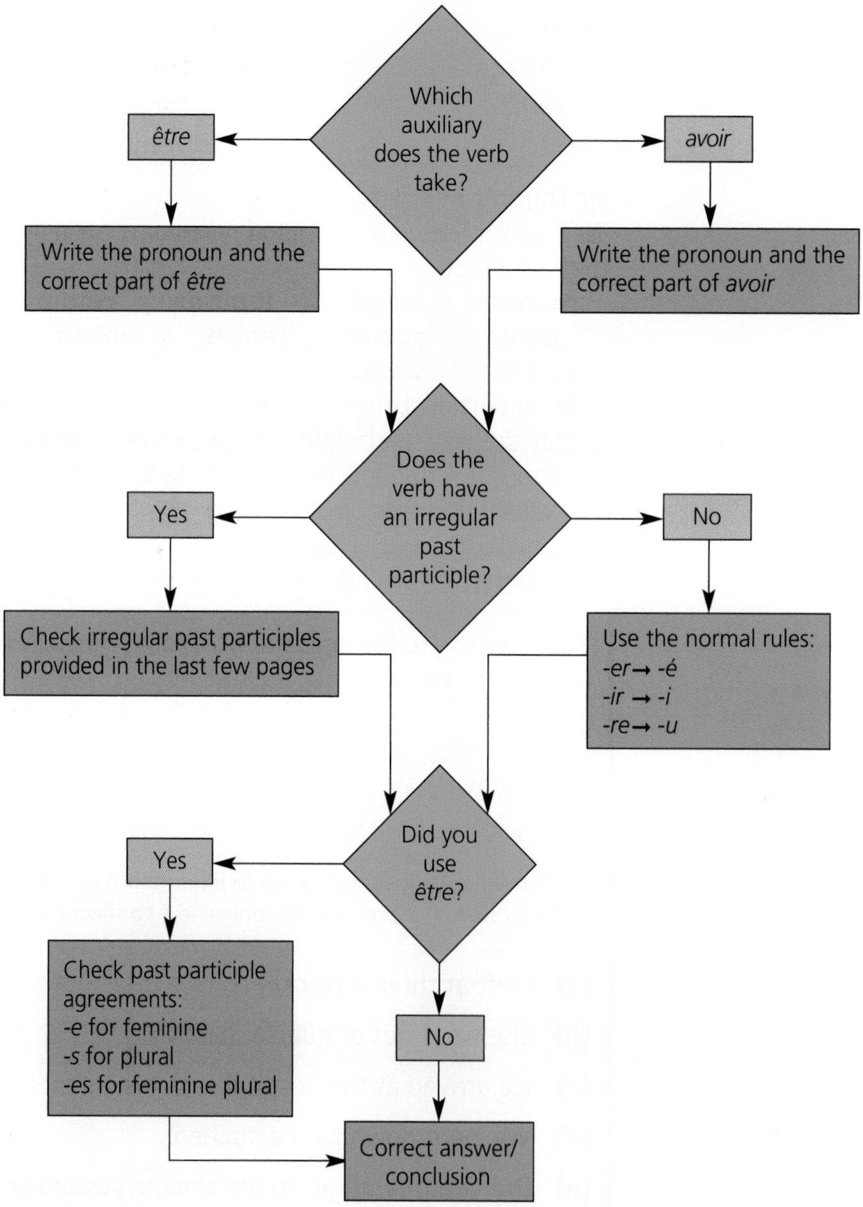

Reflexive verbs in the passé composé

Reflexive verbs in the **passé composé** have four sections, for example:

je me suis lavé	I washed myself

Reflexive verbs in the **passé composé** are formed in the same way as the verbs that use **être** as an auxiliary but they have the reflexive pronoun as well. For example, here is **se laver** (to wash oneself/to have a wash):

je me suis lavé(e)	I washed myself
tu t'es lavé(e)	you washed yourself
il s'est lavé	he washed himself
elle s'est lavée	she washed herself
nous nous sommes lavé(e)s	we washed ourselves
vous vous êtes lavé(e)(s)	you washed yourselves
ils se sont lavés	they (m.) washed themselves
elles se sont lavées	they (f.) washed themselves

Beware the irregular reflexive verb **s'asseoir** (to sit down), which becomes **je me suis assis.**

Test yourself 15

Translate the following sentences into French. The infinitive of each verb is shown at the end of each sentence. Answers are given at the back of the book.

Example:
I had a shower at seven o'clock. (**se doucher**)
Je me suis douché(e) à sept heures.

(a) She got dressed in her bedroom. (**s'habiller**)
(b) Pierre broke his leg. (**se casser**)
(c) He washed in the bathroom. (**se laver**)
(d) We went to bed after the film. (**se coucher**)
(e) They (*feminine*) had an argument. (**se disputer**)
(f) They (*masculine*) went for a walk in the park. (**se promener**)
(g) You (*singular*) got up very early. (**se lever**)
(h) You (*plural*) ran away last year. (**se sauver**)
(i) We (*feminine*) sat down under a tree. (**s'asseoir**)

Level 2

The imperfect tense

The imperfect tense translates 'was', 'were' and 'used to'. It expresses what was happening or what used to happen, or describes what someone or something was like.

Knowledge of the imperfect tense is not essential for Level 1 in Common Entrance but you will need to recognise it in Level 2. The following phrases will be useful:

c'était	it was
c'était amusant	it was fun
il y avait	there was, there were
il faisait beau	the weather was fine
il faisait mauvais	the weather was bad
j'étais content(e)	I was pleased
il/elle était en vacances	he/she was on holiday

To form the imperfect, use the **nous** form of the present tense of the verb and take off the **-ons** ending. Then add the following endings:

je	-ais	nous	-ions
tu	-ais	vous	-iez
il	-ait	ils	-aient
elle	-ait	elles	-aient

For example:

Present:	nous allons	nous mangeons	nous faisons
Imperfect:	j'allais	je mangeais	je faisais

Examples:

I was playing the trumpet.	**Je jouais** de la trompette.
He used to go skiing.	**Il faisait** du ski.

Être is the only verb that does not follow the rule. Note that each conjugation of the verb begins with **ét-** followed by the necessary ending:

j'étais	I was	nous étions	we were
tu étais	you were	vous étiez	you were
il/elle était	he/she was	ils/elles étaient	they were
c'était	it was		

Test yourself 16

Translate the following sentences into French. Answers are given at the back of the book.

Example:
I was chatting with my friends.
Je bavardais avec mes amis.

(a) He was listening to some music.
(b) We were watching TV.
(c) They (*feminine*) used to work on a farm.
(d) They (*masculine*) used to play cricket.
(e) You (*singular*) were reading a letter in the office.
(f) Were you (*plural*) listening to the radio?
(g) It was cold. (Use **faire**.)
(h) She used to be a teacher.

Interrogative

There are various ways to turn a statement into a question in French, but the following are the easiest:

1 Simply add a question mark to any statement and, if you are speaking, change your intonation, for example:

Tu vas en ville. (You are going to town.)

Tu vas en ville? (Are you going to town?)

Note that we have listed some useful question phrases in the section on the Speaking paper in the Introduction.

2 Put **Est-ce que** (**Est-ce qu'** before a vowel) in front of the statement, for example:

Est-ce que tu vas en ville?

Est-ce qu'il va en ville?

Negatives

The most common negative is 'not'; other commonly used negatives are 'never', 'nothing' and 'no longer'.

Part A

ne … pas	not	ne … plus	no longer, not any more
ne … rien	nothing	ne … jamais	never

Notes:

1 **Ne … pas, ne … rien**, etc. go around the verb, for example:

Je **ne** vais **pas**.	I am **not** going.
Elle **n'**aime **pas** …	She does **not** like …

Notice that ne becomes n' in front of a verb beginning with a vowel or a silent h.

2 In the **passé composé, ne … pas** goes around the auxiliary, for example:

Elle **n'**a **pas** mangé.	Je **ne** suis **pas** tombé.

3 With two verbs together, **ne … pas** goes around the first verb, for example:

Je **n'**aime **pas** jouer au netball.	Il **ne** veut **pas** danser.

4 Remember that **pas** (along with other negative phrases) is not followed by **un, une** or **des**. It is only followed by **de** or **d'**, for example:

Je **n'**ai **pas de** gomme.	I do not have a rubber.
Il **n'**a **plus d'**eau.	He does not have any more water.

Test yourself 17 ✓

Translate the following sentences into English. Answers are given at the back of the book.

Example:
Je ne joue pas au tennis.
I do not play tennis.

(a) Je n'ai rien mangé.
(b) Elle n'est pas contente.
(c) Nous n'avons pas vu les lions.
(d) Il ne boit jamais de limonade.
(e) Nous n'avons plus de bananes.

Here are some more negatives (which are not essential for Common Entrance, although you will need to be able to recognise **ne … personne** in Level 2). Read the notes that follow carefully.

Part B

ne … personne	nobody, not anyone	ne … que	only
ne … aucun(e)	none, not any	ne … ni … ni …	neither ... nor

Notes:

1 These negative words go round the whole verb even in the **passé composé** or when two verbs are together, for example:

Je **ne** vois **aucun** problème.	I do not see any problem.
Elle **n'**a vu **personne**.	She saw nobody.
Je **ne** vais voir **personnne**.	I am not going to see anyone.

2 **Personne ne** can start a sentence, for example:

Personne ne sait.	Nobody knows.
Personne n'est venu.	Nobody came.

3 **Ne … que** means 'only'. **Que** comes directly before the word to which it refers, for example:

Je **ne** vais à l'église **que** le dimanche.	i.e. I do not go to church any day other than Sunday.
Je **ne** vais **qu'**à l'église le dimanche.	i.e. I do not go anywhere other than church on Sundays.

4 **Jamais**, **rien** and **personne** can be used alone as one-word answers, for example:

Qui est là? Personne.	Who is there? Nobody.

Test yourself 18 ✓

Translate the following sentences into English. Answers are given at the back of the book.

Example:

Je n'ai que trois crayons.

I only have three pencils.

(a) Nous n'avons vu personne.

(b) Personne ne comprend le passage.

(c) Je n'ai vu ni Pierre ni Louise.

(d) Nous n'allons au cinéma que le samedi soir.

(e) Il ne va qu'à son café préféré.

1.2 Pronouns

Glossary of terms:

Pronoun This is a word used instead of a noun, e.g. 'I', 'me', 'he', 'she', 'it', 'them'.

Subject The subject can be a noun or a pronoun and is the person or object doing a particular thing.

Object A direct object is the person, animal or thing that receives an action. An indirect object is when you say 'to me', 'to him', etc., e.g.:

Subject	**Verb**	**Direct object**
I	am eating	cake
Subject	**Verb**	**Indirect object**
He	is speaking	to her

Subject pronouns and object pronouns

Subject		Direct object		Indirect object	
je, j'	I	me, m'	me	me, m'	to me
tu	you	te, t'	you	te, t'	to you
il	he, it	le, l'	him, it	lui	to him
elle	she, it	la, l'	her, it	lui	to her
on	one	–	–	–	–
nous	we	nous	us	nous	to us
vous	you	vous	you	vous	to you
ils	they	les	them	leur	to them
elles	they	les	them	leur	to them

Note that j', m', t', l' are used before a vowel. For example: j'arrive, je l'ai vu.

Order of object pronouns

All object pronouns go before the verb, or before the auxiliary verb in the passé composé.

Je **le** vois	I see **him/it**
Nous **l'**adorons	We love **him/her/it**
Je **lui** ai parlé	I spoke **to him/her**
Il **m'**a rencontré	He met **me**

Two more useful object pronouns: y and en

The word **y** means 'there' and it goes in front of the verb like the other object pronouns:

Il va au cinéma demain après-midi?	Is he going to the cinema tomorrow afternoon?
Non, il **y** va demain matin.	No, he is going **there** tomorrow morning.

The word **en** means 'of it', 'of them', 'some' or 'any' and replaces a phrase beginning with **de**, **du**, **de la**, **de l'** or **des**, for example:

Tu as combien de frères?	How many brothers do you have?
J'en ai trois.	I have three (**of them**).
J'ai mangé des bonbons.	I ate some sweets.
J'en ai mangé.	I ate **some**.

Relative pronouns qui and que

Level 1 candidates are only required to know qui (who), whereas **Level 2** candidates should be able to use que as well.

Qui and **que/qu'** are relative pronouns that translate 'who', 'whom', 'which' or 'that'.

'Who' is always translated by **qui**, whereas 'whom' is usually translated by **que** (see the examples that follow). Note however that prepositional phrases such as 'for whom', 'with whom', 'without whom' are translated by **pour qui**, **avec qui**, **sans qui**.

When deciding whether to use **qui** or **que**, note that **qui** will normally be directly followed by the verb, whereas **que** will normally be followed by a noun or subject pronoun, for example:

Le garçon qui est dans la voiture est mon cousin.	The boy who is in the car is my cousin.
Le livre qui était dans mon sac a disparu.	The book that was in my bag has disappeared.
Le garçon que tu as vu est mon cousin.	The boy whom/that you saw is my cousin.
Le livre que j'ai lu hier soir est bon.	The book that I read yesterday evening is good.
Le chien qu'elle préfère est le terrier.	The dog that she prefers is the terrier.

1.3 Nouns

Glossary of terms:

Noun A noun is used to name a person, a place, an object or an abstract quality such as politeness.

Singular A noun is singular when there is only one of it, e.g. 'boy', 'child', 'car'.

Plural A noun is plural when there are more than one of them, e.g. 'boys', 'children', 'cars'.

Gender All nouns in French are either masculine or feminine. The gender of a word may be different from what might be expected in English.

Article The definite article in English is 'the'. The indefinite article in English is 'a' or 'an'.

Definite and indefinite articles

English	Masculine singular	Feminine singular	Singular nouns beginning with a vowel or **h**	All plurals
a, an	**un**	**une**	**un** or **une**	
the	**le**	**la**	**l'**	**les**
some	**du**	**de la**	**de l'**	**des**
of the, from the	**du**	**de la**	**de l'**	**des**
to the, at the	**au**	**à la**	**à l'**	**aux**

Nouns in the plural

To make a French noun plural, you usually add **-s**, for example **un chien, deux chiens.**

If the noun ends in **-al**, change it to **-aux**, for example **un animal, des animaux.**

If the noun ends in **-eau**, change it to **-eaux**, for example **un chapeau, des chapeaux.**

Test yourself 19 ✓

Look at the words below, paying particular attention to whether they are masculine or feminine, then fill in the blanks. Answers are given at the back of the book.

dog: **chien** (m.) house: **maison** (f.) shop: **magasin** (m.)
hotel: **hôtel** (m.) cheese: **fromage** (m.) water: **eau** (f.)
apple: **pomme** (f.)

(a) a dog

_____ **chien**

(b) the house

_____ **maison**

(c) some shops

_____ **magasins**

(d) some water

_____ **eau**

(e) some cheese

_____ **fromage**

(f) an apple

_____ **pomme**

(g) some apples

_____ **pommes**

(h) to the shops

_____ **magasins**

(i) to the house

_____ **maison**

(j) at the hotel

_____ **hôtel**

(k) the name of the dog

le nom _____ **chien**

(l) at the shops

_____ **magasins**

Translating 'some' and 'of'

The word 'some' can be translated by **du**, **de la**, **de l'** or **des**, for example:

du fromage	de la confiture	de l'eau	des oranges

If the noun is preceded by a quantity, **du**, **de la**, **de l'** and **des** change to just **de** or **d'** (before a vowel or a silent **h**), for example:

du fromage	*but*	un kilo de fromage	a kilo of cheese
de la confiture	*but*	un pot de confiture	a jar of jam
des chocolats	*but*	une boîte de chocolats	a box of chocolates
de l'eau	*but*	une bouteille d'eau	a bottle of water
des bonbons	*but*	un paquet de bonbons	a packet of sweets

The same rule applies after the word **pas**, for example:

J'ai des livres. I have some books.	*but*	Je n'ai pas de livres. I do not have any books.
Avez-vous des croissants? Do you have some croissants?	*but*	Nous n'avons pas de croissants. We do not have any croissants.

Other important uses of au, du and de la after jouer

In English we say 'I play football' and 'I play the piano'.

In French we differentiate between sport and musical instruments, using **jouer au** and **jouer du/de la**:

je joue au rugby	je joue du piano
je joue au tennis	je joue du violon
je joue au foot	je joue de la flûte
	je joue de la clarinette

1.4 Adjectives

Glossary of terms:

Adjective An adjective describes a noun. In French, adjectives must agree with the noun that they are describing; that is to say, they must be singular or plural, masculine or feminine.

Agreement Adjectives and some past participles in French change their ending to make them feminine or plural.

Comparative This is when two or more things are compared; so one thing is said to be 'bigger' or 'faster' or 'more expensive' than another.

Superlative This is when you are saying that something is the 'biggest' or 'slowest' or 'most expensive' out of a group of things.

For example: un **grand** garçon, une **grande** fille, trois **grands** garçons, deux **grandes** filles.

The general rules for agreement are:

masculine singular: no change	masculine plural: add -s
feminine singular: add -e*	feminine plural: add -es

*Unless the word ends in -e anyway, for example: rouge, jaune, orange.

The following adjectives do not follow these rules.
Adjectives ending in **-eux** change to **-euse**:

Masculine	Feminine	English
dangereux	dangereuse	dangerous
délicieux	délicieuse	delicious
heureux	heureuse	happy
joyeux	joyeuse	happy/joyful
paresseux	paresseuse	lazy

Adjectives ending in **-f** change to **-ve**:

Masculine	Feminine	English
actif	active	active
neuf	neuve	brand new
sportif	sportive	sporty

Adjectives ending in **-n** change to **-nne**:

Masculine	Feminine	English
ancien	ancienne	old
bon	bonne	good

Adjectives ending in **-er** change to **-ère**:

Masculine	Feminine	English
premier	première	first

These common adjectives do not follow any rules so they have to be learnt:

Masculine	Feminine	English
beau*	belle	beautiful/handsome
blanc	blanche	white
gentil	gentille	kind
gros	grosse	fat
long	longue	long
nouveau*	nouvelle	new
vieux*	vieille	old

*Note that before a masculine noun beginning with a vowel or a silent h, these change to bel, nouvel, vieil.

For example: un bel homme, un vieil arbre.

The position of adjectives

Most adjectives come **after** the noun they are describing. This includes colours, for example **un chien blanc, des chaussures noires.** There are 17 exceptions. This rhyme will help you remember the adjectives that come **before** the noun:

mauvais, méchant, vilain, beau,
petit, haut, vieux, joli, gros,
nouveau, gentil, jeune et bon,
grand, meilleur, vaste et long.

For example: **un petit chien noir, une belle maison blanche.**

Some adjectives change their meaning depending on whether they are before the noun or after it:

ancien

un ancien élève	a former pupil
un bâtiment ancien	an ancient building

cher (m.), **chère** (f.)

un cher ami	a dear (male) friend
une chère amie	a dear (female) friend
un chapeau cher	an expensive hat
une chemise chère	an expensive shirt

même

la même chemise	the same shirt
le jour même	the very day

pauvre

pauvre Pierre	poor Pierre
une famille pauvre	a poor family

propre

sa propre chambre	his/her own bedroom
sa robe propre	her clean dress

Look at the following sentences and notice the positions of the adjectives and the gender of each one:

1 Mon **meilleur** ami a une **grande** voiture **rouge**.

2 Je suis assez **grosse** car je ne suis pas **sportive** et je suis un peu **paresseuse**.

3 Le **jeune** homme a les cheveux **courts** et **frisés**.

4 Ma **nouvelle** amie est **grande** et elle est très **gentille**.

5 Le **petit** chien **blanc** est **méchant**.

Test yourself 20 ✓

Fill in the blanks, making sure the adjective agrees with the noun. Answers are given at the back of the book.

(a) a red dress

une robe _____

(b) a delicious ice cream

une glace _____

(c) a good story

une _____ histoire

(d) a kind lady

une _____ dame

(e) a little brown mouse

une _____ souris _____

(f) some intelligent pupils

des élèves _____

(g) an old house

une _____ maison

Test yourself 21 ✓

Translate the following, making sure you think about whether the adjectives go before or after the noun, as well as thinking about agreements. Answers are given at the back of the book.

(a) a big black horse
(b) a little sister
(c) long hair (*remember hair is always plural!*)
(d) dear Julie
(e) an expensive T-shirt
(f) a pretty girl
(g) brown shoes
(h) an intelligent teacher

Comparison of adjectives

plus … que	more … than	moins … que	less … than
aussi … que	as … as		

For example:

Je suis plus intelligent(e) que mon frère.	I am more intelligent than my brother.
Elle est moins grande que moi.	She is less tall than me.
Elle est aussi grande que son frère.	She is as tall as her brother.

The superlative

The superlative form of adjectives translates 'the most …' or 'the …est', for example 'the biggest', 'the most intelligent'.

When using the superlative you just need to know the gender of the noun you are describing, then use the correct word for 'the', add the word **plus** and an adjective with an appropriate agreement, for example:

Marc est **le plus** petit de la classe.	Marc is the smallest in the class.
Marie et Claire sont **les plus** intelligentes.	Marie and Claire are the cleverest.
La plus jolie fille s'appelle Anne.	The prettiest girl is called Anne.

Possessive adjectives

Masculine singular	Feminine singular	All plurals	English
mon	ma	mes	my
ton	ta	tes	your
son	sa	ses	his, her, its
notre	notre	nos	our
votre	votre	vos	your
leur	leur	leurs	their

Note that if a feminine noun begins with a vowel or a silent h, you use the masculine form for 'my', 'your' (singular), 'his', 'her', 'its'.

For example: **mon** école (my school), **son** église (her church, his church).

Remember: It is the gender of the following noun that is important. It does not matter if you are a boy or a girl!

For example: **sa** mère (his mother), **sa** mère (her mother).

Test yourself 22

✓

Translate the following phrases into French. Answers are given at the back of the book.

Examples:

my brother	her sister
mon frère	*sa sœur*
his sister	their parents
sa sœur	*leurs parents*

(a) our house

(b) your (*polite*) aunt

(c) his mother

(d) her cats

(e) our children

(f) your (*singular*) bedroom

(g) their school

(h) my grandmother

Demonstrative – this, these

Masculine singular	Masculine singular in front of a vowel or **h**	Feminine singular	All plurals
ce	cet	cette	ces

For example:

ce livre	this book	cette maison	this house
cet homme	this man	ces livres	these books

1.5 Adverbs

Glossary of terms:

Adverb An adverb describes how somebody does something.

Formation of adverbs

1 Most adverbs are formed from a corresponding adjective. To form an adverb from the adjective, make the adjective feminine and add **-ment** at the end, for example:

Masculine adjective	Feminine adjective	Adverb	English for the adverb
doux	douce	doucement	gently
malheureux	malheureuse	malheureusement	unfortunately

A common exception:

Masculine adjective	Feminine adjective	Adverb	English for the adverb
gentil	gentille	gentiment	kindly

2 If the masculine adjective ends in a vowel, add **-ment** to the masculine form, for example:

facile	easy	**facilement**	easily

3 If the masculine adjective ends in **-ant**, the adverb ends in **-ammant**, for example:

constant	constant	**constammant**	constantly

4 If the masculine adjective ends in **-ent**, the adverb ends in **-emment**, for example:

récent	recent	**récemment**	recently

An exception to this is **lent** (slow), which becomes **lentement** (slowly).

5 Sometimes the final **-e** of the feminine form of the adjective becomes **-é**, for example:

énorme	huge	**énormément**	hugely

6 Not all French adverbs are formed in this way. Some just have to be learnt:

beaucoup	a lot	**peu**	little, not much
bien	well	**tard**	late
longtemps	for a long time	**tôt**	early
loin	far	**vite**	quickly
mal	badly		

Position of adverbs

Adverbs normally come after the verb, for example:

Il marche lentement.	He walks slowly.

Most adverbs come after the past participle in the **passé composé**:

L'homme a conduit dangereusement.	The man drove dangerously.

However, a few common adverbs go between the auxiliary and the past participle, for example:

J'ai bien dormi.	I slept well.
J'ai mal dormi.	I slept badly.
Il a trop bu.	He drank too much.

1.6 Prepositions

Glossary of terms:

Preposition A preposition is a word used to show the relationship between two nouns, for example: The cat sat **under** the table.

Common prepositions are:

après	after	sauf	except
avant	before	sous	under
avec	with	sur	on
chez	to/at the house of	vers	towards
contre	against	à part	apart from
dans	in	autour de*	around
depuis	since	à côté de*	next to
derrière	behind	en dehors de*	outside of
devant	in front of	en face de*	opposite
en	in, by, while, made of	au milieu de*	in the middle of
entre	between	près de*	near
malgré	in spite of	à cause de*	because of
par	by, through	loin de*	far from
pendant	during	à gauche de*	on the left of
pour	for	à droite de*	on the right of
sans	without		

*Note that de may need to change. If the next word is masculine, de changes to du. If the next word is plural, de becomes des.

For example: à côté du mur, près des magasins.

Test yourself 23 ✓

Translate the following phrases into French. Answers are given at the back of the book.

Examples:

near the post office — *près de la poste*

next to the cinema — *à côté du cinéma*

(a) on the left of the butcher's

(b) at Simon's house

(c) behind the market

(d) during the match

(e) opposite the church

(f) under the table

(g) on the chest of drawers

(h) next to the bank

(i) with my friends

(j) in the classroom

It is worth mentioning here disjunctive, or emphatic, pronouns, which are the pronouns that follow prepositions, for example 'with me', 'for you', 'without him', 'behind us'.

moi	me	nous	us
toi	you	vous	you
lui	him	eux	them (m.)
elle	her	elles	them (f.)

Tu viens **avec moi**?	Are you coming with me?
Voici un cadeau **pour toi**.	Here is a present for you.
Nous allons **avec lui**.	We are going with him.

Test yourself 24

Translate the following phrases into French. Answers are given at the back of the book.

(a) without me
(b) for him
(c) behind you (*singular*)
(d) before us
(e) with her
(f) to their house

1.7 Conjunctions

Glossary of terms:

Conjunction Conjunctions are linking words such as 'and' or 'but'.

Conjunctions link sentences together. Common examples are:

ainsi	therefore	et	and
alors	so	mais	but
aussi	also	ou	or
car	because	parce que/qu'	because
donc	so	puis	then
ensuite	then	si	if

2 Tackling the Writing paper

As mentioned in the Introduction, there are four parts in the Level 1 Writing paper:

Section 1

This question will require you to write six items of vocabulary on a specific topic.

Section 2

This question will be a grammar multiple-choice exercise.

Section 3

This question will require you to write short sentences about five pictures.

Section 4

This question will require you to write a few short sentences on a given topic from the syllabus.

As mentioned in the Introduction, there are two parts to the Level 2 Writing paper:

Level 2

Section 1 (10 marks)

This question will require you to translate five sentences into French. Each sentence is worth 2 marks. Nouns and genders will be given, as well as infinitives of verbs and the masculine singular of adjectives. The verbs **avoir** and **être** will not be given and you will be expected to insert other words as necessary. The past tense will not be needed in this question.

Level 2

Section 2 (15 marks)

This question will require 80–120 words of continuous writing in the form of an email. Five bullet points will be provided in French and English, and you will need to write about at least four of them. You will be expected to demonstrate the full range of your knowledge of the linguistic features contained in the syllabus. In order to access the top marks, you will need to be able to use the past, present and near future. Marks are awarded for content, accuracy and quality of language.

How to succeed in Level 1

Section 1

- In Section 1, you will have to write six things from the topic mentioned in the instructions.
- There will be pictures to help you but they are only a suggestion. This means that you can write the French words for the pictures provided or for other things from the same topic.
- You do not need to write **un**, **une**, **le**, **la**, **l'** or **les**.

Section 2

This is a grammar section, in which you will have to choose the correct missing word to complete each sentence. Each missing word will be a verb or an adjective.

Here is an example:

Complete the following sentence by selecting the correct form of the verb or adjective from those given in the brackets.

Elle ______________ la musique. (adorent, adore, adorons)

The answer is **adore** because this is the **Elle** form of the verb, ending in **-e**.

Section 3

To gain a good mark in Section 3 of Level 1, you will need to write a simple but very accurate sentence for each picture. You must make sure that what you write is relevant to the picture, but you can be quite flexible in your interpretation of it. Let's look at an example:

Maybe you have forgotten how to say 'to play cards' in French. Do not worry!

Look at some of the things you could write:

- **J'aime inviter mes amis chez moi.**

  I like to invite my friends to my house.
- **Voici mon ami Paul, ma sœur Marie et moi.**

  This is my friend Paul, my sister Marie and me.

Do not be afraid of simplicity but, if you can, try to vary the tenses you use in your sentences and show different structures. In each of the sentences in the previous example, you would have impressed your examiner with an infinitive phrase in the first sentence and good use of possessive pronouns in the second. In neither have we used the phrase **jouer aux cartes**, but now that you know it, here is a third example:

- **Je joue aux cartes avec mes amis dans la cuisine.**

  I play cards with my friends in the kitchen.

Try to write between 5 and 10 words per sentence. Do not worry if you exceed 10 words and write 11 or 12, but avoid going beyond that. The more you write, the more likely you are to make a mistake! On the other hand, if you write only 5 words for each sentence, you are not giving yourself a real chance to show what you know.

Here is another example:

Here are some possible answers:

• Voici mon père avec notre chien.	Here is my father with our dog.
• Papa aime promener le chien tous les jours.	Dad likes to walk the dog every day.
• J'aime faire des promenades avec mon chien Bruno.	I like going for walks with my dog Bruno.
• Quand il fait beau, je promène le chien dans le parc.	When the weather is fine, I walk the dog in the park.
• Mon chien, qui s'appelle Rufus, est très mignon.	My dog, who is called Rufus, is very cute.
• Est-ce que tu aimes les chiens?	Do you like dogs?
• Tu veux promener le chien avec moi?	Do you want to walk the dog with me?
• Nous avons un grand chien, brun et blanc.	We have a big brown and white dog.

Note that there are a couple of questions among these sentences. It adds a little bit of interest to your writing. Try to include one in your exam.

Section 4

Here is an example of the type of question that you will be asked to complete in Section 4 of Level 1:

Write five short sentences in French about your town – *ma ville*.
(*Try to avoid repetition and copying from other parts of the paper.*)

As in the Section 3 question, you will need to write five simple but accurate sentences, and you must make sure that what you write is relevant to the topic.

Here are some possible sentences in response to the above question:

- J'habite dans la banlieue de York.
- C'est une grande ville historique dans le nord de l'Angleterre.
- Il y a une cathédrale magnifique ici.
- Beaucoup de touristes aiment visiter York.
- Près de York, la campagne est très jolie.

How to succeed in Level 2

Level 2 Section 1

Here is an example of a Level 2 Section 1 type of question:

> Use the vocabulary provided to help you translate the following sentence into French.
>
> I cannot go out this evening because I have a lot of homework to do.
>
> pouvoir, sortir, soir (m.), devoir (m.), faire

You will see that some French words are provided below the English sentence. You have to use these words to build the sentence in French.

Remember:

- Not all of the words are provided – you will have to fill in the rest yourself.
- Verbs are given to you in the infinitive ('to …') so you will have to put them in the correct form.
- Nouns are given to you in the singular form and you are told the gender. The gender is particularly important if you have to use an adjective.
- You must write the words in the correct order and therefore think about things like where adjectives go.

> The correct translation of the above example is:
>
> Je ne <u>peux</u> pas <u>sortir</u> ce <u>soir</u> parce que j'ai beaucoup de <u>devoirs</u> à <u>faire</u>.
>
> The underlined words are the ones provided below the English sentence. In the translation, **pouvoir** has changed to the je form: **peux**; and the singular noun **devoir** has changed to the plural: **devoirs**.

Level 2 Section 2

Here is an example of a Level 2 Section 2 type of question:

> Write an email in French to a French friend. You should write between 80 and 120 words. You must mention at least four of the following points:

• Une activité que tu aimes	An activity that you like
• Un week-end typique chez toi	A typical weekend at your home
• Une description de tes vacances	A description of your holidays
• Le week-end dernier	Last weekend
• Demain	Tomorrow

The key to this kind of exercise is planning. Begin by asking yourself questions about the bullet points. Here are the points in English from the example above, with key question words beside them:

• An activity that you like	What? When? With whom? Why? How long? Cost?
• A typical weekend at your home	What? When? With whom? Where?
• A description of your holidays	Where? When? With whom? Weather? Travel? Activities?
• Last weekend	Activities? Cost? Where? When? Why? With whom?
• Tomorrow	Activities? With whom? When? Where?

By asking yourself questions about the bullet points, you can form an idea in your head about what you want to write. Once you have this, you need to think about how you are going to write the email.

You may not feel able yet to write about all these things. The following chapters will give you lots of vocabulary and phrases to help you, as well as lots of questions to practise with. You could have a go at writing this email when you have completed Chapter 8.

How to write an email

Level 2

*The opening and finishing sentences should not be included in your 80–120 word count, but they help to make a good impression.

Cher Marc,
Chère Anne,
*Opening sentence(s) **
Answer the questions/do the task as asked
*Finishing sentence(s) **
Amitiés

Your name

Opening sentences:

Merci de ton e-mail que j'ai reçu hier matin.	Thank you for your email, which I received yesterday morning.
Je suis content(e) de savoir que tu vas bien.	I am pleased to know that you are well.
Ici nous allons tous très bien.	We are all very well here.
Je veux te parler de …	I want to tell you about …

Finishing sentences:

En attendant de tes nouvelles.	Waiting to hear your news.
Écris-moi vite.	Write back quickly.
Amitiés/Amicalement	Best regards (literally 'friendly greetings')
Bises/Bisous	Kisses (note that the French never sign off with xxx)

You now have the ideas and the structure but need to put it all together.

Expanding your sentences

The following ideas should help you expand your sentences to make your writing more interesting. Think beyond the verb! Add details such as **when** you did something, **where**, **with whom**, **why**, **how you went there**, **what it was like.** Here are a couple of examples of how to expand your writing:

Example A:

1 **Je suis allé(e) à la plage.**

I went to the beach.

2 **Hier après-midi je suis allé(e) à la plage.**

Yesterday afternoon I went to the beach.

3 **Hier après-midi je suis allé(e) à la plage avec mes parents.**

Yesterday afternoon I went to the beach with my parents.

4 **Hier après-midi il faisait très chaud alors mes parents et moi avons décidé d'aller à la plage.**

Yesterday afternoon it was very hot so my parents and I decided to go to the beach.

5 **Hier après-midi, il faisait très chaud, alors, après le déjeuner, mes parents et moi avons décidé d'aller à la plage qui est à dix minutes en bus de notre hôtel. J'ai nagé dans la mer et j'ai fait un château de sable magnifique – c'était super!**

Yesterday afternoon it was very hot, so, after lunch, my parents and I decided to go to the beach, which is ten minutes by bus from our hotel. I swam in the sea and made a fantastic sandcastle – it was great!

Example B:

1 **J'ai acheté un gâteau.**
I bought a cake.

2 **Dimanche j'ai acheté un gâteau pour ma grand-mère.**
On Sunday I bought a cake for my grandmother.

3 **Dimanche c'était l'anniversaire de ma grand-mère alors je suis allé(e) à la pâtisserie acheter un gâteau.**
On Sunday it was my grandmother's birthday so I went to the cake shop to buy a cake.

4 **Dimanche je suis allé(e) à la pâtisserie acheter un grand gâteau au chocolat pour ma grand-mère car c'était son anniversaire. Cela m'a coûté quinze euros mais c'était délicieux!**
On Sunday I went to the cake shop to buy a big chocolate cake for my grandmother as it was her birthday. It cost me 15 euros but it was delicious!

You should be well on your way to forming a quality piece of writing, but you also need to think about the style. Your writing should flow well and sentences should be linked smoothly together.

On the following page is a list of connecting phrases. Learn them and use some in your email.

enfin	finally
aussi vite que possible	as quickly as possible
aussitôt que possible	as soon as possible
sans hésiter	without hesitation
sans perdre de temps	without wasting any time
vers midi	towards midday
après cela	after that
pendant une heure	for an hour
un peu plus tard	a little later
une demi-heure plus tard	half an hour later
à ce moment-là	at that moment
soudain	suddenly
malheureusement	unfortunately
par hasard	by chance
pour commencer	to begin with
bon, alors	so, then
d'abord	at first
donc	so (in other words/therefore)
ce matin vers dix heures	this morning around ten o'clock
à deux heures	at two o'clock
au bout d'un moment	some time later
peu de temps après	a short time later
tout de suite après	immediately after
tout de suite	immediately
immédiatement	immediately
deux minutes plus tard	two minutes later
à la fin de la journée	at the end of the day
vers la fin de la journée	towards the end of the day
de temps en temps	from time to time
puis	then
heureusement	fortunately
ainsi	therefore
après avoir fait cela	after doing that
je veux aussi mentionner	I would also like to mention
malgré ça	despite that

Topics and useful vocabulary

Chapters 3–9 cover all the Common Entrance topics (see 'Topics' within the Introduction for the list of CE topics), with sample CE-style questions giving you practice in the four skills. You will find lots of important vocabulary and useful phrases in each chapter to help you revise. However, these word lists are not exhaustive and we suggest you use the ISEB *French Vocabulary for Key Stage 3 and Common Entrance*, available from Galore Park, in conjunction with this book.

Some general vocabulary follows that will be useful for all the topic areas covered.

Cardinal numbers

0	zéro	13	treize	60	soixante
1	un	14	quatorze	70	soixante-dix
2	deux	15	quinze	71	soixante et onze
3	trois	16	seize	80	quatre-vingts
4	quatre	17	dix-sept	90	quatre-vingt-dix
5	cinq	18	dix-huit	91	quatre-vingt-onze
6	six	19	dix-neuf	100	cent
7	sept	20	vingt	101	cent un
8	huit	21	vingt et un	199	cent quatre-vingt-dix-neuf
9	neuf	22	vingt-deux	200	deux cents
10	dix	30	trente	202	deux cent deux
11	onze	40	quarante	1000	mille
12	douze	50	cinquante	2000	deux mille

Ordinal numbers

1st	premier (m.)	6th	sixième
1st	première (f.)	7th	septième
2nd	deuxième	8th	huitième
3rd	troisième	9th	neuvième
4th	quatrième	10th	dixième
5th	cinquième		

Days

les jours de la semaine	the days of the week	jeudi	Thursday
lundi	Monday	vendredi	Friday
mardi	Tuesday	samedi	Saturday
mercredi	Wednesday	dimanche	Sunday

Months

les mois de l'année	the months of the year	juillet	July
janvier	January	août	August
février	February	septembre	September
mars	March	octobre	October
avril	April	novembre	November
mai	May	décembre	December
juin	June		

3 Family, friends and pets

3.1 Meeting people

People

les gens (m.)	people	les ados	teenagers
la personne	person	l'enfant (m. and f.)	child
trois personnes	three people	le/la camarade	friend
l'homme (m.)	man	l'ami(e)	friend
le monsieur	gentleman	le copain	friend (m.)
la dame	lady	la copine	friend (f.)
la femme	woman, wife	le correspondant	penfriend (m.)
un(e) adolescent(e)	teenager	la correspondante	penfriend (f.)

Some useful verbs

rencontrer	to meet
retrouver	to find
se rencontrer	to meet up with one another
se retrouver	to meet up with one another
s'amuser	to have fun, enjoy oneself
s'entendre avec …	to get on with someone

Useful phrases for greeting people

Bonjour*	Hello, good morning, good afternoon
Bonsoir*	Good evening
Bonne nuit	Good night
Salut	Hi/Cheerio
Allô	Hello (only when answering the telephone)
Au revoir	Goodbye
Bonne journée	Have a good day
Bonne soirée	Have a good evening
À bientôt	See you soon

*Note that if you greet a man or woman in English, you will probably just say 'Good morning' or 'Hello', but in French you should say Bonjour Monsieur or Bonjour Madame.

Useful phrases for introductions

Je te présente ma famille	May I introduce my family? (informal)
Je vous présente ma famille	May I introduce my family? (formal)
Enchanté(e)	Pleased to meet you
Voici mon chien	This is my dog
Comment t'appelles-tu?	What is your name?
Je m'appelle …	I am called …
Comment s'appelle-t-il/elle?	What is his/her name?
Il/Elle s'appelle …	He/She is called …
Comment allez-vous?	How are you? (formal)
Je vais bien, merci	I am well, thank you
Ça va?	How are you? (informal)
Ça va	I am fine
Et toi?	What about you?

Useful phrases for arranging to meet friends

Rendez-vous où?	Where shall we meet?
On se retrouve où et à quelle heure?	Where shall we meet and at what time?
Rendez-vous au stade	Let's meet at the stadium
Rendez-vous à la piscine	Let's meet at the swimming pool
Rendez-vous devant la gare	Let's meet outside the station
À demain	See you tomorrow
À dimanche	See you on Sunday

? Exam-style questions

Try these sample exam-style questions for yourself. Answers are given at the back of the book.

Speaking

Role-play practice

Look at the section on the Speaking paper in the Introduction for help with role plays.

Level 2

3.1 Your penfriend's mother comes to visit you. Try to say the following in French. The examiner's part is also shown.

(a) Hello Mrs Duroc.
Bonjour.

(b) How are you?
Très bien, merci. Et toi?

(c) I am well thank you.
Excellent.

(d) I would like to introduce my family.
Enchantée. Et comment s'appelle ton chat?

(e) My cat is called Peggy.
Moi, j'adore les chats.

(f) Do you have a cat?
Oui, nous avons deux chats.

Level 2

3.2 Your friend Julie calls you on your mobile. Try to say the following in French. The examiner's part is also shown.

(a) Hello Julie.
Salut. Ça va?

(b) I am fine, thank you. How are you?
Ça va bien, merci. Tu veux rencontrer demain?

(c) Yes. Where shall we meet?
Près de la pharmacie?

(d) No. I prefer the railway station.
D'accord.

(e) See you tomorrow.
Oui, à bientôt.

(f) Good night.
Au revoir.

Relatives

Male relatives

le beau-père	stepfather, father-in-law	le grand-père	grandfather
le demi-frère	stepbrother, half-brother	le neveu	nephew
l'enfant (m.)	child (m.)	l'oncle (m.)	uncle
le fils	son	papa	dad
le frère	brother	le père	father
le frère aîné	the oldest brother	le petit-ami	boyfriend
le frère cadet	the youngest brother	le petit-fils	grandson
le frère jumeau	twin brother		

Female relatives

la belle-mère	stepmother, mother-in-law	la petite-amie	girlfriend
la demi-sœur	stepsister, half-sister	la petite-fille	granddaughter
l'enfant (f.)	child (f.)	la sœur	sister
la fille	daughter	la sœur aînée	the oldest sister
la grand-mère	grandmother	la sœur cadette	the youngest sister
maman	mum	la sœur jumelle	twin sister
la mère	mother	la tante	aunt
la nièce	niece		

Plural relatives

les grands-parents	grandparents	les jumeaux	twins
les petits-enfants	grandchildren		

Useful adjectives

âgé	old	marié	married
célibataire	single, unmarried	veuf, veuve	widowed
divorcé	divorced		

Test your writing

Write six sentences giving the names of members of your family.

Remember to use the words **mon, ma, mes** (my).

Examples:

Ma tante s'appelle Anne.

Mes grands-parents s'appellent Marie et Henri.

Exam-style questions

Try these sample exam-style questions for yourself. Suggested answers are given at the back of the book.

Writing

3.3 Your French friend is coming to visit you. Write a list in French of six members of your family, as in the example.

(The pictures shown are only a suggestion. You may use any relevant items of vocabulary.)

Example:

■ *mère*

Level 2

3.4 Use the vocabulary provided to help you translate the following sentences into French.

(a) My parents live in a small house at the seaside.
parent (m.), habiter, petit, maison (f.), mer (f.)

(b) The child meets his cousins behind the cinema.
enfant (m.), rencontrer, cousin (m.), cinéma (m.)

(c) We are going to my grandparents' house next week.
aller, grand-parent (m.), prochain, semaine (f.)

(d) The ladies in my family are very beautiful.
dame (f.), famille (f.), beau

(e) My mother loves to go to the theatre with her father.
mère (f.), adorer, aller, théâtre (m.), père (m.)

3.2 Describing people and pets

Character

amusant	amusing	méchant	naughty
drôle	funny	paresseux, paresseuse	lazy
dynamique	lively	patient	patient
gentil, gentille	kind	poli	polite
impatient	impatient	sociable	sociable
impoli	impolite, rude	souriant	smiling
inquiet, inquiète	worried, anxious	sympa	nice, kind
marrant	funny	travailleur, travailleuse	hard-working

Appearance

beau, belle	handsome, beautiful	joli	pretty
costaud	well-built	laid	ugly
grand	big, tall	mince	thin
gros, grosse	fat	petit	small

Useful phrases

Je m'appelle Sophie	I am called Sophie
J'ai treize ans	I am 13 years old
J'ai les cheveux courts/longs	I have short/long hair
J'ai les yeux bleus	I have blue eyes
Je suis de taille moyenne	I am medium height
Je porte des lunettes	I wear glasses
Il/Elle est grand(e)	He/She is tall
Il a douze ans	He is 12 years old

Elle a les cheveux blonds/roux/noirs	She has blonde/red/black hair
Il a les cheveux bruns	He has brown hair
Il a une barbe/Il est barbu	He has a beard
Il est chauve	He is bald
Il est roux	He is red-haired
Elle est rousse	She is red-haired
Elle est brune	She is a brunette
Elle a des tâches de rousseur	She has freckles
Je suis fille unique	I am an only child (girl)
Je suis fils unique	I am an only child (boy)
Je suis l'aîné(e)	I am the eldest
Je suis le cadet/la cadette	I am the youngest
Je suis le benjamin	I am the youngest boy
Ma sœur est plus âgée que moi	My sister is older than me
Mon frère m'énerve	My brother annoys me
Je m'entends bien avec ma sœur	I get on well with my sister

Personal details

l'adresse mail (f.)	email address	la nationalité	nationality
l'âge (m.)	age	le nom	name
la carte d'identité	identity card	le numéro de téléphone	telephone number
la date de naissance	date of birth	le passeport	passport
le lieu de naissance	place of birth	le pays d'origine	country of origin

Test your reading ✓

Select a suitable answer from the following options for each of the questions on this form:

anglais	le 12 avril 2005	Bristol
Peter Roberts	Angleterre	14 ans

Nom: ....

Âge: ....

Date de naissance: ....

Lieu de naissance: ....

Pays d'origine: ....

Nationalité: ....

Jobs

This list is not exhaustive. Check with your teacher how to describe your parents' jobs.

le métier	job, profession
acteur (m.), actrice (f.)	actor, actress
agent de police	policeman, policewoman
architecte	architect
avocat	lawyer
chômeur (m.), chômeuse (f.)	unemployed
au chômage	unemployed, out of work
comptable	accountant
conducteur d'autobus (m.), conductrice d'autobus (f.)	bus driver
dentiste	dentist
directeur (m.)	director, headmaster
directrice (f.)	director, headmistress
employé(e) de banque	bank employee
facteur (m.), factrice (f.)	postman, postwoman
femme d'affaires	businesswoman
fermier (m.), fermière (f.)	farmer
homme d'affaires	businessman
infirmier (m.), infirmière (f.)	nurse
instituteur (m.), institutrice (f.)	primary school teacher
journaliste	journalist
médecin	doctor
ouvrier (m.), ouvrière (f.)	unskilled worker
patron (m.), patronne (f.)	owner, boss
pharmacien (m.), pharmacienne (f.)	chemist
professeur	teacher
retraité(e)	retired
secrétaire	secretary
serveur (m.), serveuse (f.)	waiter, waitress
soldat	soldier
vendeur (m.), vendeuse (f.)	shop assistant

Note that when you describe somebody's job in French, you do not put un or une before the job. For example, you say:

Il est médecin. (He is a doctor.)

Examples:

Que fait ton père/ta mère comme métier?	What does your father/mother do for a living?
Il est professeur.	He is a teacher.
Je voudrais être agent de police.	I would like to be a policeman/ policewoman

Test your speaking ✓

Read these passages aloud, then describe yourself in the same way.

Je m'appelle Marc et j'ai treize ans. Je suis assez grand et très fort. J'ai les yeux bleus et les cheveux courts et blonds. J'ai une sœur qui s'appelle Anne et elle a quinze ans. Elle est intelligente mais très paresseuse. Elle n'est pas sportive mais elle adore la musique pop.

Salut! Je m'appelle Marie et j'ai douze ans. J'ai les yeux bruns et les cheveux longs et raides. Je suis fille unique mais j'ai trois labradors et deux poissons rouges. Je suis forte en biologie et je veux être dentiste. Tu aimes la télé? Moi j'adore les films.

Je m'appelle Louise et j'habite à Londres, la capitale de l'Angleterre. Il y a cinq personnes dans ma famille: mes deux parents, ma sœur Sophie, mon frère Paul et moi. Sophie et Paul sont jumeaux et ils ont six ans. Moi j'ai douze ans et je suis l'aînée.

? Exam-style questions

Try these sample exam-style questions for yourself. Suggested answers are given at the back of the book.

Speaking

Oral discussion

3.5 **(a)** Fais-moi une petite description de toi-même.

Describe yourself.

(b) Décris ta famille.

Describe your family.

(c) As-tu des frères ou des sœurs?

Do you have any brothers or sisters?

(d) Que fait ton père/ta mère comme métier?

What is your father's/mother's job?

(e) As-tu des animaux à la maison?

Do you have any animals at home?

(f) Comment est ton meilleur ami/ta meilleure amie?

What is your best friend like?

Role-play practice

Look at the section on the Speaking paper in the Introduction for help with role plays.

Level 2 ●

3.6 A French boy or girl is visiting your school. Try to say the following in French. The examiner's part is also shown.

(a) Hello. My name is …

Salut. Avec qui est-ce que tu habites?

(b) I live with my parents.

Est-ce que tu as des frères?

(c) I am an only child.

Comment est ton père?

(d) My father is tall, thin and very sporty.

Et que fait ta mère?

(e) My mother is a dentist.

Ma mère est actrice.

(f) Do you have any animals?

Oui, j'ai un chien.

Exam-style questions

Try these sample exam-style questions for yourself. Answers are given at the back of the book.

Listening

Track 1

3.7 Listen to Marc talking about himself and the members of his family and give at least two details for each one.

Person	First detail	Second detail
Marc		
Mother		
Father		
Matthieu		
Luc		
Jean		

Track 2

3.8 Listen to the man talking about his family and pick the correct answer, as in the example.

Example:
He is called *Jean-Marc*. Jean Marc Jean-Marc

(a)	In his family there are ______ people.	three	four	five
(b)	He has ______.	three boys	two girls and a boy	two boys and a girl
(c)	His wife has ______ hair.	long curly	short straight	long straight
(d)	He is ______.	an artist	an actor	a teacher
(e)	He leaves home at ______.	7.30	7.05	7.35

Clothes

le blouson	casual jacket	le sweat	sweatshirt
le foulard	scarf (silk)	le tricot	wool jumper or cardigan
le gant	glove	la chaussette (f.)	sock
le gilet	waistcoat	la chaussure (f.)	shoe
l'imperméable (m.)	raincoat	la chemise	shirt
le jean	jeans	la cravate	tie
le jogging	tracksuit	l'écharpe (f.)	scarf
le maillot	sports vest	la jupe	skirt
le maillot de bain	swimming costume/trunks	la robe	dress
le manteau	coat	la sandale	sandal
le pantalon	trousers	la veste	jacket
le pull	jumper		

Test your writing ✓

Write a list of six articles of clothing without looking at the vocabulary list. Check your answers afterwards against the vocabulary list.

Some useful verbs

essayer	to try, try on	porter	to wear
mettre	to put on (clothes)		

Description of clothes

à manches longues/courtes	long-/short-sleeved	sale	dirty
court	short	propre	clean
long, longue	long	trop petit	too small

Colours

blanc, blanche	white	noir	black
bleu	blue	rose	pink
brun	brown	rouge	red
gris	grey	vert	green
jaune	yellow		

Test your writing ✓

Test your memory. Once you have learnt the clothes in French, look around you. Can you write a description of what somebody in the room is wearing? If you are alone in the room, maybe there is a photo that you can describe.

Pets

le chat	cat	le lapin	rabbit
le chaton	kitten	l'oiseau (m.)	bird
le cheval	horse	le perroquet	parrot
le chien	dog	le poisson rouge	goldfish
le chiot	puppy	le serpent	snake
le cochon d'Inde	guinea pig	la perruche	budgie
le hamster	hamster		

Useful phrases

Je m'occupe de mon hamster	I look after my hamster
Je donne à manger au chat	I feed the cat
Je promène le chien	I walk the dog

Exam-style questions

Try these sample exam-style questions for yourself. Answers are given at the back of the book.

Reading

3.9 Match the sentences with the pictures, as in the example. Be careful as there are two spare sentences. Answers are given at the back of the book.

Example:

A4

A ~~J'ai les cheveux longs.~~

B Rendez-vous à la piscine.

C Voici ma famille.

D Mon père est dentiste.

E C'est mon anniversaire et j'ai douze ans.

F Mon chat s'appelle Mimi.

G J'ai un poisson rouge.

H Je porte un T-shirt blanc.

1

3

5

2
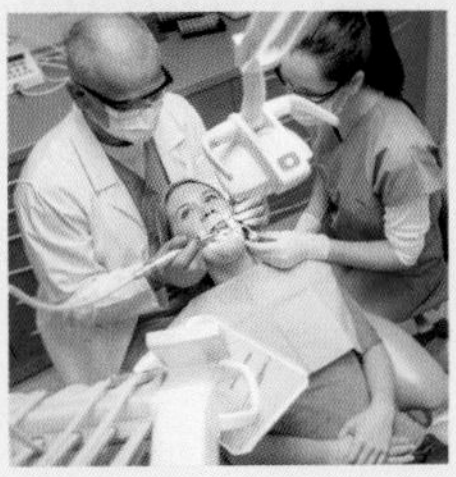

4

6

3.10 Read the following passage and find the French for the words and phrases listed below.

Je m'appelle Shrek et je suis le héros d'un film très célèbre. Je suis un grand ogre vert. On dit que je suis laid et que je sens mauvais. J'ai de grands yeux bruns mais je suis chauve. J'habite dans un marais avec ma nouvelle femme qui s'appelle Fiona. Elle est une princesse mais aussi une ogresse. Je crois qu'elle est l'ogresse la plus belle du monde. Elle a les cheveux longs et roux et les yeux verts. Elle porte une longue robe verte et, moi, je porte un gilet marron, une chemise sale, des chaussettes marron et des bottes.

(a) hero

(b) famous

(c) ugly

(d) I smell bad

(e) bald

(f) my new wife

(g) a female ogre

(h) the most beautiful in the world

(i) a waistcoat

(j) dirty

3.11 Read the following passage and answer the questions that follow in English.

Luc habite dans une ferme avec ses deux parents. Il aime habiter à la campagne parce qu'il joue avec les animaux et il aime surtout apprendre de nouveaux tours à son chien. Il y a toutes sortes d'animaux commes les vaches, les moutons, les poules et les cochons. Il aime tous les animaux sauf un. Dans un champ près de la ferme il y a un cheval qui s'appelle Rex. Il a de grands yeux bruns. Luc a peur de Rex parce qu'il chasse tous ceux qui entrent dans le champ.

Un matin, Luc était en retard pour l'école donc il a décidé d'entrer dans le champ car c'est plus rapide. Rex était très loin mais il a vu Luc et il a commencé à courir. Au milieu du champ il y a un poirier et Luc a couru au poirier et y a grimpé.

Les poires étaient mûres et Luc en a donné une à Rex. Rex l'a mangée donc Luc a eu une idée. Il a jeté une poire très loin et Rex est allé trouver la poire et l'a mangée. Luc a sauté de l'arbre et s'est échappé en courant. Il a couru jusqu'à l'école et ça c'était la dernière fois qu'il est entré dans le champ de Rex.

(a) Where does Luc live? (Give two details.)

(b) What does Luc like to do with his dog?

(c) What type of animal is Rex?

(d) Why does Luc not like Rex?

(e) Why did Luc decide to go into Rex's field?

(f) What exactly did Luc climb?

(g) How did Luc escape?

Exam-style questions

Try these sample exam-style questions for yourself. Suggested answers are given at the back of the book.

Writing

3.12 Your French friend asks whether you and your friends have any pets. Write a list in French of six possible pets, as in the example.

(The pictures shown are only a suggestion. You may use any relevant items of vocabulary.)

Example:

- *chien*

3.13 Complete the following sentences by selecting the correct form of the verb or adjective from those given in the brackets.

(a) Comment t'____________-tu? (appelle, appelles, appellent)

(b) Je m'____________ Marc. (appelle, appelles, appellent)

(c) L'enfant est ____________. (grand, grande, grands)

(d) Mes lunettes sont ____________. (brun, bruns, brunes)

(e) J'____________ à Paris. (habite, habites, habitez)

3.14 Write a sentence of between five and ten words for each picture, as in the example.

Example:

- *Ma mère joue au tennis tous les soirs en été.*

(a)

(b)

★ Make sure you know

- ★ How to greet people in formal and informal situations
- ★ How to arrange to meet people
- ★ How to give your personal details
- ★ How to describe people's appearance and character
- ★ How to talk about your family
- ★ How to talk about people's jobs
- ★ How to talk about pets
- ★ How to describe clothes

Test yourself 25 ✓

Before moving on to the next chapter, make sure you can answer the following questions. Answers, where relevant, are given at the back of the book.

Say:

1 **(a)** Hello (to your French friend).

(b) Hello (to your friend's parents).

(c) This is my sister, Stephanie.

(d) How are you?

(e) Let's meet at the swimming pool.

(f) Goodbye, see you on Saturday.

2 Read the sentences below and add either **J'ai** (I have) or **Je suis** (I am) to each one.

(a) ___ les cheveux noirs, courts et frisés.

(b) ___ les yeux verts.

(c) ___ très mince.

(d) ___ trois frères.

(e) ___ assez courageux.

(f) ___ grosse et petite.

(g) ___ onze ans.

(h) ___ sympa.

(i) ___ méchant mais poli.

(j) ___ un chien et trois poissons rouges.

3 Write a list of five masculine words and five feminine words for things to wear. Check the vocabulary lists in this chapter for your spellings.

4 House, home, daily routine and chores

J'habite ...	I live ...
dans un appartement	in a flat
dans une maison individuelle	in a detached house
dans une maison mitoyenne	in a semi-detached house
dans un pavillon	in a suburban villa
dans une ferme	on a farm
en Angleterre	in England
à Londres	in London

Ma maison se trouve ...	My house is situated ...
dans une ville	in a town, city
dans un village	in a village
dans le Dorset	in Dorset
dans la banlieue	in the suburbs
dans les environs de ...	in the suburbs of ...
à la campagne	in the country
au bord de la mer	at the seaside
au nord/au sud (de)	in/to the north/south (of)
à l'est/à l'ouest (de)	in/to the east/west (of)
sur la côte	on the coast

Ma maison est ...	My house is ...
confortable	comfortable
en brique	made of brick
en pierre	made of stone

Chez moi il y a ...	At my home there is/are ...
deux étages	two floors
au premier étage	on the first floor
au deuxième étage	on the second floor
en haut	upstairs
en bas	downstairs
le bureau	office, desk
le grenier	loft, attic
le salon	sitting room
le séjour	living room
le toit	roof
le vestibule	hallway
l'alarme (f.)	burglar alarm
la buanderie	utility room
la cave	cellar
la chambre	bedroom
la chambre d'amis	guest room
la cheminée	chimney
la cuisine	kitchen
la fenêtre	window
la pièce	room
la porte d'entrée	front door
la salle à manger	dining room

Dans la cuisine il y a ...	In the kitchen there is ...
le congélateur	freezer
l'évier (m.)	sink
le four à micro-ondes	microwave oven
le four	oven
le frigo	fridge
le lave-vaisselle	dishwasher
le robinet	tap
le verre	glass
l'assiette (f.)	plate
la casserole	saucepan
la cuisinière	cooker
la soucoupe	saucer
la tasse	cup

Dans la buanderie il y a ...	In the utility room there is ...
l'aspirateur (m.)	vacuum cleaner
le lave-linge	washing machine
la machine à laver	washing machine
le seau	bucket

Dans le salon il y a ...	In the sitting room there is ...
le canapé	sofa
le canapé-lit	sofa bed
le coussin	cushion
le fauteuil	armchair
le lecteur de CD	CD player
le tableau	painting
le vase	vase
la bibliothèque	bookcase
la cheminée	fireplace

Dans la salle à manger il y a ...	In the dining room there is ...
le buffet	sideboard
la chaise	chair
la table	table

Dans ma chambre il y a ...	In my bedroom there is ...
le chevet	bedside table
le lit	bed
l'ordinateur (m.)	computer
l'oreiller (m.)	pillow
l'ours en peluche (m.)	teddy bear
le réveil	alarm clock
le tiroir	drawer
l'armoire (f.)	wardrobe
la commode	chest of drawers
la couette	duvet
la couverture	blanket
l'étagère (f.)	shelf
la radio	radio

Test your writing ✓

Read this description of a bedroom and write a description of your own bedroom.

Ma chambre est au deuxième étage à côté de la salle de bains. Dans ma chambre il y a un petit lit et à gauche du lit il y a une grande table. Sur la table il y a mon ordinateur et mes devoirs. Mes vêtements sont dans l'armoire car je n'ai pas de commode. J'adore la musique pop et je joue de la guitare électrique qui est à droite de l'armoire. J'ai beaucoup de posters de mes chanteurs préférés et j'ai des étagères pour mes livres et mes photos.

Dans ma chambre ...	In my bedroom ...
je dors	I sleep
j'écoute de la musique	I listen to music
je fais mes devoirs	I do my homework
je lis	I read
je me repose	I rest

Dans la salle de bains il y a ...	In the bathroom there is ...
le dentifrice	toothpaste
le rasoir	razor
le savon	soap
la brosse à dents	toothbrush
la serviette	towel

Dans le jardin il y a ...	In the garden there is ...
le bassin	pond
le parterre	flowerbed
le potager	vegetable garden
l'herbe (f.)	grass
la pelouse	lawn
la plante	plant
la remise	shed
la serre	greenhouse

Other useful words	
chez moi	at my home, to my home
déménager	to move house
partager	to share

Pour aider mes parents ...	To help my parents ...
je fais le jardinage	I do the gardening
je fais le ménage	I do the housework
je fais le repassage	I do the ironing
je fais la lessive	I do the laundry
je fais la vaisselle	I do the washing-up
je fais la cuisine	I do the cooking
je fais mon lit	I make my bed
je fais du babysitting	I babysit
je fais des courses	I go shopping
je débarrasse la table	I clear the table
je donne à manger au chat	I feed the cat
j'essuie la vaisselle	I dry the dishes
je lave la voiture	I wash the car
je mets la table	I lay the table
je nettoie	I clean
je passe l'aspirateur	I vacuum
je prépare le dîner	I prepare the evening meal
je ramasse mes vêtements	I pick up my clothes
je range ma chambre	I tidy my bedroom
je tonds la pelouse	I mow the lawn

Test your speaking

Read the following passage aloud then speak about your own home in the same way.

J'habite dans une assez grande maison. Elle se trouve dans la banlieue de Portsmouth dans le sud de l'Angleterre. Au rez-de-chaussée il y a un salon, une salle à manger et une grande cuisine et au premier étage il y a ma chambre, la chambre de mes parents et une chambre d'amis. La chambre de mes frères jumeaux est au grenier. J'aime beaucoup ma chambre. Mon lit est très confortable et j'ai un bureau avec un ordinateur. Derrière la maison nous avons un joli jardin. Maman s'occupe des fleurs et Papa tond la pelouse.

Exam-style questions

Try these sample exam-style questions for yourself. Suggested answers are given at the back of the book.

Speaking

Oral discussions

4.1 (a) Comment est ta maison?

What is your house like?

(b) Où se trouve ta maison?

Where is your house?

(c) Quelles pièces y a-t-il dans ta maison?

What rooms are there in your house?

(d) Qu'est-ce qu'il y a dans ta chambre?

What is there in your bedroom?

(e) Est-ce que ta maison a un jardin? Comment est le jardin?

Does your house have a garden? What is the garden like?

(f) Décris-moi ta maison idéale.

Describe your ideal house.

(g) Qui habite ta maison?

Who lives in your house?

(h) Est-ce que tu aimes ta maison?

Do you like your house?

(i) Comment est-ce que tu t'amuses chez toi?

How do you enjoy yourself at home?

(j) Qu'est-ce que tu fais pour aider tes parents?

What do you do to help your parents?

Daily routine	
je me brosse les dents	I brush my teeth
je me couche	I go to bed
je me douche	I have a shower
je m'endors	I go to sleep
je m'habille	I get dressed
je me lave	I get washed
je me lave les cheveux	I wash my hair
je me lève	I get up
je me réveille	I wake up
j'arrive à l'école à huit heures	I arrive at school at eight o'clock
je fais mes devoirs	I do my homework
je prends un bain	I have a bath
je prends le petit-déjeuner	I have breakfast
je quitte la maison	I leave the house
je rentre chez moi	I return home
je vais à la messe	I go to church/mass

Useful time phrases	
à sept heures	at seven o'clock
à huit heures et quart	at quarter past eight
à dix heures et demie	at half past ten
à cinq heures moins le quart	at quarter to five
à six heures dix	at ten past six
à six heures moins vingt	at twenty to six

? Exam-style questions

Try these sample exam-style questions for yourself. Suggested answers are given at the back of the book.

Speaking

Role-play practice

Look at the section on the Speaking paper in the Introduction for help with role plays.

Level 2

4.2 You are staying with a French penfriend. Try to say the following in French. The examiner's part is also shown.

(a) I like my room very much.

Comment est ta chambre chez toi?

(b) My bedroom in England is very small.

Tu habites en ville?

(c) I live on a farm.

Moi, je voudrais habiter au bord de la mer.

(d) At what time do you get up?

Normalement, je me lève à huit heures trente.

(e) Can I have a bath, please?

Bien sûr.

(f) I would like to go to bed.

Bonne nuit.

Level 2

4.3 You are staying with a French penfriend and are talking to one of his/her parents. Try to say the following in French. The examiner's part is also shown.

(a) I live in a house.

Tu habites au centre-ville?

(b) I live in the suburbs of London.

Il y a combien de chambres dans ta maison?

(c) There are four bedrooms in my house.

Nous avons trois chambres et un petit jardin.

(d) There is a garden behind my house.

Qu'est-ce que tu fais pour aider tes parents?

(e) I clean the cars.

Est-ce que tu fais autre chose?

(f) Sometimes I babysit.

C'est gentil.

Test your writing

(a) Write five sentences about your daily routine on a school day.

(b) Write five sentences about your routine on Sundays.

Exam-style questions

Try these sample exam-style questions for yourself. Answers are given at the back of the book.

Listening

Track 3

4.4 Listen to the following passage and pick the phrases you hear from the list below.

(a) I wake up

(b) I have a bath

(c) I get dressed

(d) I make my bed

(e) I go downstairs

(f) I prepare breakfast

(g) I lay the table

(h) I do the vacuuming

(i) I clear the table

(j) I feed the dog

Exam-style questions

Try these sample exam-style questions for yourself. Answers are given at the back of the book.

Reading

4.5 Read the following passage and choose TRUE or FALSE for each sentence that follows it.

Ma maison est vieille et elle est en brique. Mon ami Marc habite dans une maison à la campagne. Elle est moderne mais très petite. Je préfère ma maison parce que c'est plus grand et il y a un jardin avec beaucoup de fleurs et des arbres. Au rez-de-chaussée il y a quatre pièces: la cuisine, le salon, la salle à manger et le bureau de mon père. Au premier étage, en face de ma chambre, il y a la salle de bains. À gauche de la salle de bains il y a la chambre de mes parents. Mes deux sœurs partagent une chambre au deuxième étage.

Mes parents aiment faire du jardinage et ils ont une grande remise. Il y a plusieurs parterres et un grand potager. Moi, je préfère jouer au foot avec mes amis sur la pelouse.

(a) His house is made of brick.

(b) On the ground floor of his house, there are three rooms.

(c) His bedroom is next to the bathroom.

(d) His sisters have their own bedrooms.

(e) His parents grow fresh vegetables.

(f) He enjoys playing football on the patio.

4.6 Read the following passage from Eric's diary and pick the five correct sentences that follow.

Le trente mai

Aujourd'hui, c'est mon anniversaire. J'ai treize ans mais mes parents me traitent toujours comme un bébé. J'ai un petit frère qui a deux ans et une sœur qui est plus âgée que moi. Elle est paresseuse et c'est toujours moi qui fais le ménage. Quand je me lève, je dois ranger ma chambre avant de descendre en bas pour préparer le petit-déjeuner. Maman est toujours en colère si je laisse mes vêtements par terre. Après avoir mangé, je dois faire la vaisselle mais ma sœur ne fait rien.

Le soir, je fais mes devoirs tout de suite et puis je peux regarder la télé pendant une heure. Quand Papa rentre à la maison, il aide Maman dans la cuisine. Après le dîner, je dois faire la vaisselle encore une fois et Papa essuie la vaisselle. Maman dit toujours que ma sœur ne doit rien faire car elle a beaucoup de devoirs.

Eric

Example:
C'est son anniversaire. ✓

(a) Il y a quatre personnes dans la famille.

(b) Eric est l'enfant le plus âgé.

(c) Sa sœur est un bébé.

(d) Sa sœur ne fait rien.

(e) Maman est toujours fâchée s'il ne range pas ses vêtements.

(f) Eric doit ramasser ses vêtements.

(g) Sa mère fait la vaisselle.

(h) Eric fait ses devoirs avant le dîner.

(i) Papa aide Eric dans la cuisine après le dîner.

(j) Sa sœur essuie la vaisselle.

Exam-style questions

Try these sample exam-style questions for yourself. Suggested answers are given at the back of the book.

Writing

4.7 Your French friend asks what your bedroom is like. Write a list in French of six things in your bedroom, as in the example.

(The pictures shown are only a suggestion. You may use any relevant items of vocabulary.)

Example:

- *lit*

4.8 Complete the following sentences by selecting the correct form of the verb or adjective from those given in the brackets.

(a) Ma maison est ____________. (grand, grande, grands)

(b) Le salon est ____________. (petit, petite, petites)

(c) La machine à laver est ____________. (blanche, blanc, blancs)

(d) Luc ____________ ses vêtements. (ramasse, ramasses, ramassent)

(e) Maman ____________ le petit-déjeuner. (préparent, préparez, prépare)

4.9 Write a sentence of between five and ten words for each picture.

(a)

(b)

Level 2

4.10 Use the vocabulary provided to help you translate the following sentences into French.

(a) She is doing her homework in front of the television.

faire, devoir (m.), télévision (f.)

(b) My father is brushing his teeth in the bathroom.

père (m.), se brosser, dent (f.), salle de bains (f.)

(c) My sister is preparing her lunch in the kitchen.

sœur (f.), préparer, déjeuner (m.), cuisine (f.)

(d) I mow the big lawn with my brother each week.

tondre, grand, pelouse (f.), frère (m.), semaine (f.)

(e) In my bedroom I have six large posters and three small plants.

chambre (f.), grand, poster (m.), petit, plante (f.)

Level 2

4.11 Your penfriend is going to visit you in June. Write an email of 80–120 words. You must mention at least four of the following points:

- Où tu habites — Where you live
- Une description de ta maison — A description of your house
- Le jardin — The garden
- Hier soir — Yesterday evening
- Demain matin — Tomorrow morning

★ Make sure you know

★ How to explain where you live

★ How to describe where you live

★ How to describe the rooms in your home

★ How to describe your daily routine

★ How to talk about what you do to help at home

Test yourself 26 ✓

Before moving on to the next chapter, make sure you can answer the following questions. Answers, where relevant, are given at the back of the book.

1 Copy and complete with the correct French verb:

(a) J'______ à Londres.

(b) Ma chambre ______ en face de la chambre de ma sœur.

(c) Mon frère ______ la table.

(d) Je me ______ les dents dans la salle de bains.

2 Copy and complete the grid below with five items that you may find in each of the rooms. Pay particular attention to the gender of the words. Check your answers by looking at the vocabulary lists earlier in the chapter.

Dans la cuisine	Dans le salon	Dans ma chambre

5 In town, travel and transport, food and drink

5.1 Description of a town, directions and shopping

Main buildings and places in town

le centre-ville	town centre
l'hôpital (m.)	hospital
l'hôtel de ville (m.)	town hall (in a large town)
l'office de tourisme (m.)	tourist office
le parking	car park
le stade	stadium
la cathédrale	cathedral
l'école (f.)	school
l'église (f.)	church
la gare	railway station
la gare routière	bus station
la gendarmerie	police station
la mairie	town hall (in a small town or village)
la piscine	swimming pool
la place principale	main square
la station de métro	underground station

Around the town or region

le banc	bench	le piéton	pedestrian
le bâtiment	building	le pont	bridge
le bois	wood	le trottoir	pavement
le bruit	noise	la banlieue	suburbs
le carrefour	crossroads	la circulation	traffic
le champ	field	la queue	queue
l'embouteillage (m.)	traffic jam	la rue	street, road
les feux (m.)	traffic lights	la zone piétonne	pedestrianised area
le jardin public	park	sens interdit	no entry
le panneau	road sign	sens unique	one way
le parc	park	toutes directions	all routes
le passage à niveau	level crossing		

Town adjectives

animé	busy	fermé	closed
calme	quiet	ouvert	open

Directions

allez	go
continuez	continue
descendez	go down/get off/get out of (bus, train, car)
montez	go up/get in/get on (bus, train, car)
devant	in front of
derrière	behind
entre	between
prenez	take
tournez	turn
traversez	cross
en face (de ...)	opposite
juste après	just after
sous	under
sur	on
la première à gauche	the first on the left
la deuxième à droite	the second on the right
tout droit	straight ahead, straight on
à 2 kilomètres d'ici	2 kilometres from here
à 200 mètres du cinéma	200 metres from the cinema

Useful phrases

Où se trouve ...?	Where is ...?
Où est ...?	Where is ...?
C'est où?	Where is it?
Pour aller à ...?	How does one get to ...?
C'est loin d'ici	It is far from here
C'est près d'ici	It is near here

Examples:

Excusez-moi, Monsieur, pour aller à la poste, s'il vous plaît?

Excuse me, Sir, how do I get to the post office, please?

Descendez la rue et prenez la deuxième à gauche.

Go down the street and take the second on the left.

Où se trouve la gare, Madame?

Where is the railway station, Madam?

C'est en face de la mairie.

It is opposite the town hall.

Pour aller au cinéma, s'il vous plaît?

How do I get to the cinema, please?

Prenez le bus numéro trois et descendez à la place principale.

Take the number three bus and get off at the main square.

Types of shops

le centre commercial	shopping centre
le grand magasin	department store
le kiosque	kiosk (for newspapers or ice cream)
le magasin de jouets	toy shop
le marchand de fruits et légumes	greengrocer
le pressing	dry cleaner's
le supermarché	supermarket
le tabac	tobacconist's (where you can buy postcards and newspapers)
l'agence immobilière (f.)	estate agency
l'agence de voyages (f.)	travel agency
l'animalerie (f.)	pet shop
la bijouterie	jeweller's shop
la boucherie	butcher's
la boulangerie	baker's
la boutique de cadeaux	gift shop
la charcuterie	delicatessen
la confiserie	sweet shop
la crémerie	dairy
l'épicerie (f.)	grocer's
la librairie	book shop
la papeterie	stationer's (for stationery, not newspapers)
la pâtisserie	cake shop
la poissonnerie	fishmonger's

Shopping

l'argent (m.)	money	le rayon des vêtements	clothes department
l'argent de poche (m.)	pocket money	la cliente (f.)	customer
le client (m.)	customer	la promotion	special offer
le panier	basket	les soldes (f.)	the sales
le rayon fromage	cheese counter	la vitrine	shop window

Useful shopping phrases

Avez-vous …?	Do you have …?
Je voudrais …	I would like …
Et avec ça?	Anything else?
C'est tout, merci	That's all, thanks
Combien?	How much?/How many?
C'est combien?	How much is that?
Ça fait dix euros	That comes to 10 euros
Je n'ai pas de monnaie	I do not have any change
J'ai seulement un billet de cinquante euros	I only have a 50 euro note
Merci beaucoup	Thank you very much

Shopping verbs

dépenser	to spend	passer à la caisse	to go to the checkout
faire la queue	to queue	peser	to weigh
faire du lèche-vitrine	to go window shopping	servir	to serve

At the tourist office

la carte de la région	map of the area
la liste des hôtels	list of hotels
la liste des campings	list of campsites
des renseignements sur …	some information about …

Useful phrases

Pouvez-vous me donner …?	Can you give me …?
Qu'est-ce qu'il y a à faire?	What is there to do?
Qu'est-ce qu'il y a à voir?	What is there to see?
Qu'est-ce qu'il y a comme distractions?	What is there to do?
La piscine ouvre à quelle heure?	At what time does the swimming pool open?
Le supermarché ferme à quelle heure?	At what time does the supermarket close?

In a bank or post office

le bureau	office	la carte bancaire	bank card
le chèque	cheque	signer	to sign
le colis	parcel	la livre sterling	British pound
le facteur	postman	envoyer	to send
le paquet	package	poster	to post
le timbre	stamp	retirer de l'argent	to withdraw money
la boîte aux lettres	letter box		

Exam-style questions

Try these sample exam-style questions for yourself. Suggested answers are given at the back of the book.

Speaking

Oral discussions

5.1 **(a)** Qu'est-ce qu'il y a comme distractions près de chez toi?

What is there to do near your home?

(b) Tu aimes faire du shopping?

Do you like shopping?

(c) Où est-ce qu'on achète de la viande/des bonbons/une glace?

Where do you buy meat/sweets/an ice cream?

Role-play practice

Look at the section on the Speaking paper in the Introduction for help with role plays.

Level 2

5.2 You are at a bank. Try to say the following in French. The examiner's part is also shown.

(a) I would like to change some money.

Qu'est-ce que vous avez?

(b) I have pounds sterling.

Qu'est-ce que vous voudriez?

(c) I would like 200 euros.

Vous avez votre passeport?

(d) Yes, I have my passport.

Voilà.

(e) Is the bank open on Saturdays*?

Oui, jusqu'à midi.

(f) At what time does the bank open on Mondays*?

À neuf heures.

*Note that 'on Saturday' is just samedi, but 'on Saturdays' is le samedi. This applies to all the days of the week of course.

For example: Qu'est-ce que tu fais dimanche? (What are you doing on Sunday?)

Je ne vais pas à l'école le dimanche. (I do not go to school on Sundays.)

Level 2

5.3 You are in town. Try to say the following in French. The examiner's part is also shown.

(a) Where is the supermarket?

Au bout de la rue.

(b) Is it called Carrefour?

Oui, le supermarché s'appelle Carrefour.

(c) Is it far from here?

C'est à deux minutes d'ici à pied.

(d) Is it the big building on the right?

Oui.

(e) Is there a post office nearby?

C'est à gauche du supermarché.

(f) Is there a letter box nearby?

Oui, c'est devant la poste.

Exam-style questions

Try these sample exam-style questions for yourself. Answers are given at the back of the book.

Listening

Track 4

5.4 Listen to these people and choose the place where they should go.

(a)	tourist office	post office	bank
(b)	tourist office	post office	bank
(c)	bakery	cake shop	delicatessen
(d)	fishmonger's	chemist's	butcher's
(e)	church	school	town hall

Track 5

5.5 Listen to the conversation and choose TRUE or FALSE for each sentence below, as in the example.

Example:
Anne a 13 ans.
True

(a) Anne reçoit de l'argent de poche.

(b) Anne range la chambre de ses parents.

(c) Anne fait le ménage.

(d) Papa fait des courses.

(e) Anne n'aime pas faire du shopping.

Exam-style questions

Try these sample exam-style questions for yourself. Answers are given at the back of the book.

Reading

5.6 Read the sentences below and work out the position of each place in the town.

(a)	La banque	(b)	L'épicerie	(c)
		La rue		
(d)	La poste	(e)	(f)	(g)

- Le cinéma est en face de l'épicerie.
- La boulangerie se trouve entre le cinéma et la poste.
- Le supermarché est à côté de la poste.
- La pharmacie est à côté de la banque mais elle n'est pas à côté de l'épicerie.
- La librairie est en face de la boulangerie.
- La poissonnerie se trouve à côté de l'épicerie.
- La pâtisserie est à côté du cinéma mais elle n'est pas à côté de la poste.

5.7 Read the sentences below, then choose the correct person's name to answer each question, as in the example.

Example:

Who is going to the chemist's? *Marie*

Marie va à la pharmacie. Elle a mal à la tête.

Philippe joue au foot dans le parc.

Amélie travaille à la charcuterie tous les samedis.

Jean fait des courses en ville.

Anne achète des timbres à la poste.

Pierre est facteur.

(a) Who works at the weekend?

(b) Who is a postman?

(c) Who does the shopping?

(d) Who plays sport?

(e) Who needs some stamps?

Exam-style questions

Try these sample exam-style questions for yourself. Suggested answers are given at the back of the book.

Writing

Level 2

5.8 Your French friend is coming to stay with you. Write a list in French of six places in your town, as in the example.

(The pictures shown are only a suggestion. You may use any relevant items of vocabulary.)

Example:

- *école*

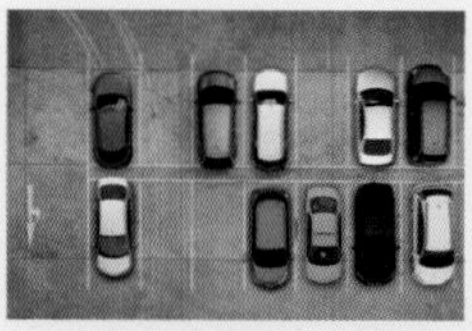

Level 2

5.9 Use the vocabulary provided to help you translate the following sentences into French.

(a) The chemist's is opposite the old church in town.

pharmacie (f.), vieux, église (f.), ville (f.)

(b) I would like a packet of yellow sweets, please.

vouloir, paquet (m.), jaune, bonbon (m.)

(c) Take the first road on the left after the cinema.

prendre, premier, rue (f.), gauche, cinéma (m.)

(d) The school is closed during the holidays.

école (f.), fermé, vacances (f.)

(e) There is a big car park in front of the swimming pool.

grand, parking (m.), piscine (f.)

5.2 Using transport

Types of transport

l'avion (m.)	plane	le vélo	bicycle
le bateau	boat	le vélomoteur	moped
le bus	bus	la bicyclette	bicycle
le camion	lorry	la camionnette	van
le car	coach	la moto	motorbike
le métro	underground	la voiture	car

Note that to say 'by car', 'by bike', etc. you generally use **en** if you sit **in** it and **à** if you sit **on** it.

For example: **à bicyclette** (by bike), **en car** (by coach), **en voiture** (by car), **à pied** (on foot).

At the railway station

le TGV (train à grande vitesse)	high-speed train
la consigne	left luggage kiosk
la douane	customs
la place	seat
la salle d'attente	waiting room
la voie	track
accès aux quais	access to the platforms
autres directions	other directions
deuxième classe	2nd class
première classe	1st class
direct	direct
en retard	late
occupé	taken, occupied (of a seat)
acheter un billet	to buy a ticket

Travelling to France

l'Eurotunnel (m.)	the 'Shuttle'
l'Eurostar (m.)	Eurostar
le tunnel sous la Manche	the Channel Tunnel
le ferry	ferry
la Manche	the English Channel
la traversée	crossing
Douvres	Dover
traverser	to cross

Useful phrases

C'est libre?	Is it free? (talking about a seat)
C'est le train pour Paris?	Is this the train for Paris?
Le train est direct?	Is the train direct?
Non, il faut changer à Paris	No, you have to change at Paris
Oui, c'est direct	Yes, it is direct
Le train part à quelle heure?	At what time does the train leave?
Le train arrive à quelle heure?	At what time does the train arrive?
C'est quel quai, s'il vous plaît?	Which platform, please?
Un aller-retour	A return ticket
Un aller simple	A single ticket

? Exam-style questions

Try these sample exam-style questions for yourself. Suggested answers are given at the back of the book.

Speaking

Oral discussions

5.10 (a) Quel est ton moyen de transport préféré?

What is your favourite type of transport?

(b) Est-ce que tu préfères voyager en bateau ou en avion? Pourquoi?

Do you prefer to travel by boat or by plane? Why?

(c) À ton avis, quel est le moyen de transport le plus confortable?

In your opinion, what is the most comfortable type of transport?

Role-play practice

Look at the section on the Speaking paper in the Introduction for help with role plays.

Level 2

5.11 You are at the railway station. Try to say the following in French. The examiner's part is also shown.

(a) I would like a second-class ticket to Paris, please.

Bien sûr. Un aller simple?

(b) No, a return ticket.

Voilà.

(c) At what time does the next train leave?

À dix heures quinze.

(d) From which platform does it leave?

Du quai numéro quatre.

(e) At what time does the train arrive in Paris?

Le train arrive à onze heures quarante.

(f) Do I have to change?

Non, c'est direct.

Level 2

5.12 You are again at the railway station. Try to say the following in French. The examiner's part is also shown.

(a) I would like to go to Lille tomorrow.

D'accord. Vous pouvez prendre le train.

(b) Is there a train at about midday?

Oui, il y a un train à midi trente.

(c) Does it arrive in Lille before 2 p.m.?

Oui, le train arrive à une heure vingt-deux.

(d) That is very fast.

Oui, et c'est très confortable.

(e) Is it direct?

Oui, c'est direct.

(f) I would like a single ticket, please.

Voilà.

Level 2

5.13 You are on the telephone to the parent of your French friend. Try to say the following in French. The examiner's part is also shown.

(a) I am travelling by bus.

Tout va bien?

(b) The bus is late.

À quelle heure est-ce que le bus va arriver?

(c) The bus is going to arrive at 11 a.m.

Où est-ce que tu vas arriver?

(d) I am going to arrive in front of the church.

C'est combien pour un billet?

(e) The ticket costs 10 euros.

C'est cher.

(f) See you soon.

Au revoir.

On the road

le chauffeur	driver	le stationnement	parking
le conducteur	driver	le véhicule	vehicle
le frein	brake	la ceinture de sécurité	seat belt
le garagiste	garage worker	l'essence (f.)	petrol
le gazole	diesel	l'huile (f.)	oil
le moteur	motor	la station-service	petrol station
le péage	toll	faire le plein	to fill up with petrol
le pneu	tyre	crevé	punctured
le sans-plomb	unleaded petrol		

Verbs

annuler	to cancel	rater	to miss
arriver	to arrive	réparer	to repair
conduire	to drive	stationner	to park
partir	to leave/depart	tomber en panne	to break down
quitter	to leave		

Exam-style questions

Try these sample exam-style questions for yourself. Suggested answers are given at the back of the book.

Writing

Level 2

5.14 Use the vocabulary provided to help you translate the following sentences into French.

(a) I have to buy four tickets for my family.

devoir, acheter, billet (m.), famille (f.)

(b) The next train leaves at what time?

prochain, train (m.), partir, heure (f.)

(c) Mum parks our red car in front of the big statue.

stationner, rouge, voiture (f.), grand, statue (f.)

(d) One can buy yellow flowers at the supermarket.

pouvoir, acheter, jaune, fleur (f.), supermarché (m.)

(e) Henri likes to read books at the library.

aimer, lire, livre (m.), bibliothèque (f.)

Level 2

5.15 You are on holiday near Paris. Write an email of 80–120 words to your cousin in Montreal. You must mention at least four of the following points:

- Ton moyen de transport préféré — Your preferred mode of transport
- Le voyage en France — The journey to France
- Des amis — Some friends
- Un incident inattendu hier — An unexpected incident yesterday
- Demain matin — Tomorrow morning

5.3 Meals and eating out

Meat

l'agneau (m.)	lamb	le veau	veal
le bœuf	beef	la dinde	turkey
le canard	duck	l'entrecôte (f.)	rib steak
le jambon	ham	le coq au vin	chicken cooked in wine
le lapin	rabbit	le steak-frites	steak and chips
le poulet	chicken		

Seafood

le poisson	fish	les fruits de mer (m.)	seafood
le crabe	crab	la bouillabaisse	fish stew (Mediterranean speciality)
le homard	lobster	la sardine	sardine
le saumon	salmon	la truite	trout
le thon	tuna	les moules (f.)	mussels

Vegetables

le champignon	mushroom	les petits-pois (m.)	peas
le chou	cabbage	le riz	rice
le chou de Bruxelles	sprout	la courgette	courgette
le chou-fleur	cauliflower	la laitue	lettuce
le concombre	cucumber	la pomme de terre	potato
le maïs	sweetcorn	les pommes de terre	potatoes
l'oignon (m.)	onion	la tomate	tomato

Fruit

l'abricot (m.)	apricot	la framboise	raspberry
l'ananas (m.)	pineapple	l'orange (f.)	orange
le citron	lemon	la pêche	peach
le melon	melon	la poire	pear
la banane	banana	la pomme	apple
la cerise	cherry	la prune	plum

Snacks and treats

un sandwich au jambon	a ham sandwich
un sandwich au fromage	a cheese sandwich
un croque-monsieur	a toasted cheese and ham sandwich
un croque-madame	a croque-monsieur with egg on top
des chips (m.)	crisps
des frites (f.)	chips
des bonbons (m.)	sweets
le gâteau	cake
le gâteau au chocolat	chocolate cake
le gâteau d'anniversaire	birthday cake

Drinks

l'apéritif (m.)	drink before a meal	le thé citron	lemon tea
le café crème	coffee with cream	le thé au lait	tea with milk
le café au lait	white coffee	le thé nature	tea without milk
le champagne	champagne	le vin blanc	white wine
le chocolat chaud	hot chocolate	le vin rouge	red wine
le chocolat froid	cold chocolate	la boisson	drink
le cidre	cider	l'eau (f.)	water
le jus de fruit	fruit juice	la limonade	lemonade
le lait	milk		

Expressions of quantity

beaucoup de	a lot of	un pot de	a pot of, a jar of
cent grammes de	100 grams of	un verre de	a glass of
plusieurs	several	une bouteille de	a bottle of
quelques	a few	une cuillère de	a teaspoon of
un bol de	a bowl of	une douzaine de	a dozen of
un demi-kilo de	a half kilo of	une portion de	a portion of
un demi-litre de	a half litre of	une tasse de	a cup of
un morceau de	a piece of	une tranche de	a slice of
un peu de	a little of		

Note that de only changes if it is followed by a noun beginning with a vowel or a silent h, when it becomes d'.

Test your writing ✓

From the vocabulary lists in this chapter, choose suitable items of food or drink to fill in the blanks.

Example:
un verre de *limonade*

(a) un pot de ____________

(b) un kilo de ____________

(c) une tasse de ____________

(d) une bouteille de ____________

(e) une portion de ____________

(f) un morceau de ____________

In the café/restaurant

le menu à prix fixe	fixed-price meal	la carte	the menu
le pourboire	tip	la nappe	tablecloth

Meals

le déjeuner	lunch	le plat principal	main course
le dessert	dessert	le repas	meal
le dîner	dinner	le souper	supper
le goûter	afternoon tea	l'entrée (f.)	starter
le petit-déjeuner	breakfast	Bon appétit!	Enjoy your meal!

English breakfast

le bacon	bacon	le yaourt	yoghurt
l'œuf à la coque (m.)	boiled egg	la baguette	French stick
l'œuf sur le plat (m.)	fried egg	la confiture	jam
le pain	bread	la confiture d'oranges	marmalade
le pain perdu	French toast	la gaufre	waffle
le petit-déjeuner anglais	English breakfast	les céréales (f.)	cereal
le porridge	porridge	les œufs brouillés (m.)	scrambled eggs
le toast	toast		

Starters

le pâté	paté	la soupe	soup
le potage	soup	les escargots (m.)	snails

Cheese and desserts

le fromage	cheese
le fromage de chèvre	goat's cheese
la glace à la fraise	strawberry ice cream
la glace à la vanille	vanilla ice cream
la glace au chocolat	chocolate ice cream
la mousse au chocolat	chocolate mousse
la tarte aux pommes	apple tart
la tarte aux fraises	strawberry tart

Useful phrases

J'ai faim	I am hungry
J'ai soif	I am thirsty
Qu'est-ce que tu prends comme plat?	What are you having as a main course?
Qu'est-ce que tu prends comme dessert?	What are you having for dessert?
Qu'est-ce qu'il y a comme boisson?	What is there to drink?
Je prends …	I will have, I am having … (food/drink)

Test your writing ✓

You are in charge of all the meals today! Write three lists of what you will have for breakfast, lunch (three courses) and dinner (three courses). Do not forget to add drinks.

? Exam-style questions

Try these sample exam-style questions for yourself. Suggested answers are given at the back of the book.

Speaking

Oral discussions

5.16 (a) À quelle heure est-ce que tu prends le petit-déjeuner?

At what time do you eat breakfast?

(b) Quel est ton fruit préféré?

What is your favourite fruit?

(c) Quelle est ta viande préférée?

What is your favourite meat?

(d) Qu'est-ce que tu aimes manger comme sandwich?

What type of sandwich do you like to eat?

(e) Qu'est-ce que tu aimes boire avec ton déjeuner?

What do you like to drink with your lunch?

Role-play practice

Look at the section on the Speaking paper in the Introduction for help with role plays.

Level 2

5.17 You are in a café. Try to say the following in French. The examiner's part is also shown.

(a) I would like a table near the window.

Vous voulez quelque chose à boire?

(b) I would like a lemonade and an apple juice, please.

Et à manger?

(c) I would like some melon, please.

Et après ça?

(d) I will have chicken and chips.

Merci.

(e) What do you have for dessert?

Nous avons beaucoup de glaces.

(f) Two vanilla ice creams, please.

Oui, tout de suite.

Level 2

5.18 You are in a restaurant. Try to say the following in French. The examiner's part is also shown.

(a) I would like a table for five people, please.

Ici?

(b) Not near the door.

D'accord. Voici votre table.

(c) The table is dirty.

Désolé(e). Je vais nettoyer la table.

(d) My parents would like a bottle of red wine.

Et qu'est-ce que vous voulez boire?

(e) I would like a glass of lemonade.

Oui, un verre de limonade.

(f) I do not have a serviette.

Je vais chercher une serviette de table.

Exam-style questions

Try these sample exam-style questions for yourself. Answers are given at the back of the book.

Reading

5.19 Read the phrases below and match each one to the correct picture, as in the example.

Example:

Une bouteille de limonade

Picture 1

1

3

5

2

4

6

(a) Une tasse de thé

(b) Un verre d'eau

(c) Une tranche de gâteau

(d) Un pot de confiture

(e) Une douzaine d'œufs

5.20 Read the three menus and answer the question that follows.

LE BOSQUET

Entrée au choix

Soupe à l'oignon
Salade au chèvre chaud
Escargots de Bourgogne

Plat au choix

Confit de canard, purée
Faux filet au poivre
Saumon, légumes

Dessert

Tarte Tatin aux pommes
Glaces et sorbets chantilly

CHEZ PIERRE

Entrée au choix

Carpaccio de bœuf
Soufflé au fromage
Terrine rustique

Plat au choix

Terrine de saumon aux epinards – Riz spécial
Fricassée de mer et sa julienne de légumes

Dessert

Poire Belle-Hélène
Mousse au chocolat

LE PETIT LAPIN

Entrée au choix

Avocat et œufs à la mousse de crabe
Quiche lorraine

Plat au choix

Côte de veau flambée à la crème
Steak – frites – salade

Dessert

Crème caramel
Gratin de fruits rouges

Which menu offers each type of food listed below? Copy and complete the grid by putting a tick to show where each type of food is available.

	Le Bosquet	Chez Pierre	Le Petit Lapin
Chips			
Duck			
Rice			
Egg			
Goat's cheese			
Apple			

Exam-style questions

Try these sample exam-style questions for yourself. Suggested answers are given at the back of the book.

Writing

5.21 Your French friend is coming to stay with you. Write a list in French of six things your friend could eat, as in the example.

(The pictures shown are only a suggestion. You may use any relevant items of vocabulary.)

Example:

■ *sandwich*

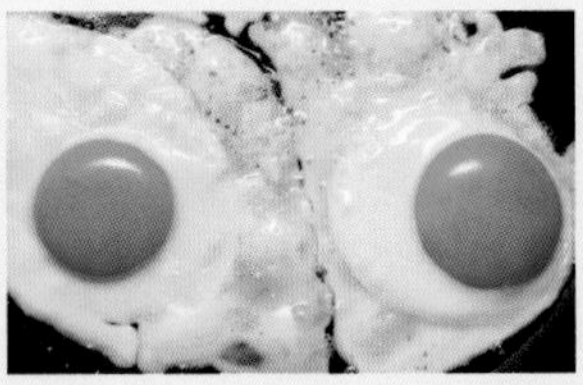

5.22 Complete the following sentences by selecting the correct form of the verb or adjective from those given in the brackets.

(a) Je voudrais une ________ bouteille de limonade, s'il vous plaît. (petite, petit, petits)

(b) Tu voudrais un chocolat ________ ? (chaud, chaude, chaudes)

(c) Il ________ un sandwich au fromage. (voudrais, voudrait, voudraient)

(d) Elle ________ une grande tranche de pizza. (manges, mangeons, mange)

(e) Je ________ une tarte aux pommes, s'il vous plaît. (prenons, prend, prends)

5.23 Write a sentence of between five and ten words for each picture.

(a) 

(b) 

(c) 

Level 2

5.24 Use the vocabulary provided to help you translate the following sentences into French.

(a) I love salmon but I do not like trout.

adorer, saumon (m.), aimer, truite (f.)

(b) I would like a ham sandwich for my sister.

vouloir, jambon (m.), sandwich (m.), sœur (f.)

(c) Mum buys a dozen croissants in town.

acheter, douzaine (f.), croissant (m.), ville (f.)

(d) Dad prefers tea with milk but I hate hot drinks.

préférer, thé (m.), lait (m.), détester, chaud, boisson (f.)

(e) Bananas are yellow but strawberries are red.

banane (f.), jaune, framboise (f.), rouge

Level 2

5.25 Write an email of 80–120 words to your penfriend describing a recent day out in another town. You must mention at least four of the following points:

• Le petit-déjeuner chez toi	Breakfast at your house
• Le voyage	The journey
• La ville	The town
• Un repas au restaurant	A meal at the restaurant
• Une prochaine excursion	A future outing

★ Make sure you know

- ★ How to describe the buildings, shops and main features of a town
- ★ How to give and understand directions
- ★ How to hold a conversation in a shop, post office and tourist office
- ★ How to talk about travel and transport
- ★ How to order food in a café or restaurant
- ★ How to talk about meals and the things you like to eat and drink

Test yourself 27

Before moving on to the next chapter, make sure you can answer the following questions. Answers, where relevant, are given at the back of the book.

1 Look at these signs and try to match them with the descriptions that follow.

1

2

3

4

5

6

7

8

9

10

11

12

13

14

15

Can you find these signs?

(a) Antiques

(b) Bakery

(c) Beware of the dog (×2)

(d) Cake shop

(e) 24 hours

(f) Danger of death (×2)

(g) Exit

(h) Fires forbidden

(i) Kitchen

(j) Stop

(k) Toilets (×2)

(l) Veterinary surgeon

2 Suggest, in French, a mode of transport for:

(a) going to the shops in your village or town

(b) going to school five miles away

(c) crossing the English Channel

(d) visiting Paris

(e) visiting the USA.

3 Write down the French for ten drinks and then check the vocabulary lists in this chapter. Make sure that you include le, la or l'.

4 How many expressions of quantity can you name in 30 seconds? Time yourself and check the list earlier in this chapter.

6 Free time

Likes and dislikes

j'aime	I like	je préfère	I prefer
j'aime surtout	I especially like	je n'aime pas	I do not like
j'adore	I love	ce que j'aime le plus	what I like the most

Indoor sports and activities

jouer au badminton	to play badminton	cuisiner	to cook
jouer au ping-pong	to play table tennis	danser	to dance
jouer au squash	to play squash	dessiner	to draw
faire de la danse	to go dancing	écouter mon lecteur MP3	to listen to my MP3 player
faire de la gymnastique	to do gymnastics	faire de la photographie	to do photography
faire du patin	to go skating	jouer aux cartes	to play cards
bavarder avec des amis	to chat with friends	jouer aux échecs	to play chess
		jouer sur l'ordinateur	to play on the computer
bricoler	to do DIY	peindre	to paint
coudre	to sew	regarder la télévision	to watch television

Outdoor sports and activities

jouer au basket	to play basketball
jouer au cricket	to play cricket
jouer au netball	to play netball
aller à la pêche	to go fishing
faire de l'alpinisme	to go climbing
faire de l'athlétisme	to do athletics
faire de l'équitation	to go horse-riding
faire du cross	to do cross-country running
faire du cheval	to go horse-riding
faire du sport	to play sport
faire du VTT	to go mountain biking
faire de la natation	to go swimming
faire de la voile	to go sailing
faire une promenade	to go for a walk
faire une randonnée	to go on a hike
promener le chien	to walk the dog

General sport vocabulary

le ballon	ball	le spectateur	spectator
le champion	champion	l'équipe (f.)	team
le concours	competition	attraper	to catch
le joueur	player	courir	to run
le match	match	participer (à)	to participate (in)

Examples:

Le sport ne m'intéresse pas.	Sport does not interest me./I am not interested in sport.
Le netball m'intéresse beaucoup.	Netball interests me a lot.
Je passe tout mon temps libre à … (infinitive)	I spend all of my free time …

Music

chanter	to sing	jouer du violoncelle	to play the cello
chanter dans une chorale	to sing in a choir	jouer de la batterie	to play the drums
jouer du clavier	to play the keyboard	jouer de la flûte	to play the flute
jouer du piano	to play the piano	jouer de la flûte à bec	to play the recorder
jouer du saxophone	to play the saxophone	jouer de la guitare	to play the guitar
jouer du violon	to play the violin	jouer de la trompette	to play the trumpet

Reading

l'auteur (m.)	author	le titre	title
l'écrivain (m.)	author	l'autobiographie (f.)	autobiography
le journal	newspaper	la BD (bande dessinée)	comic, comic strip
le magazine	magazine	l'histoire (f.)	story
le roman d'amour	romantic novel	la lecture	reading
le roman policier	detective novel	lire	to read

How often?

tous les jours	every day	en semaine	during the week
le mercredi	on Wednesdays	pendant les vacances	during/in the holidays
le week-end	at the weekend		

Useful phrases

C'est génial	It is fantastic
C'est marrant	It is funny
C'est pénible	It is tedious
Mon chanteur préféré est ...	My favourite male singer is ...
Ma chanteuse préférée est ...	My favourite female singer is ...
Ma chanson préférée est ...	My favourite song is ...
Mon groupe préféré est ...	My favourite group is ...
Il s'agit de ...	It is about ...
Ça se passe ...	It takes place ...
C'est l'histoire de ...	It is the story of ...

Test your speaking ✓

Read the following passages aloud, then try to say a few things about your own hobbies and free-time interests.

Salut! Je m'appelle Tom et je suis très sportif. J'adore jouer au rugby et j'en fais quatre fois par semaine. Il y a un match tous les mercredis après-midi et la semaine dernière nous avons gagné. Pendant les vacances je fais du VTT avec mes amis à la campagne et j'adore ça, surtout quand il pleut.

Je m'appelle Annette et je déteste le sport. Je préfère la lecture et j'aime surtout lire les romans. De temps en temps je lis un magazine mais en ce moment je lis un roman d'amour. Il s'agit d'un soldat allemand qui aime une belle fille et ça se passe en France en 1942.

Bonjour, je m'appelle Juan et je suis espagnol mais j'habite en Angleterre. Tu joues d'un instrument de musique? Moi, je joue de la trompette depuis trois ans et j'adore le jazz. Il y a un orchestre à mon école mais normalement on joue de la musique classique qui ne m'intéresse pas.

As-tu vu le western hier soir à la télé? Moi, je crois que les cowboys sont amusants. Je regarde la télé tous les soirs sauf le dimanche quand je vais dîner chez mes grands-parents.

Exam-style questions

Try these sample exam-style questions for yourself. Suggested answers are given at the back of the book.

Speaking

Oral discussions

6.1 (a) **Qu'est-ce que tu fais quand tu es libre?**

What do you do in your free time?

(b) **Quels sports pratiques-tu?**

Which sports do you do?

(c) **Quel est ton sport préféré?**

What is your favourite sport?

(d) **Quel genre de musique est-ce que tu préfères et pourquoi?**

What type of music do you prefer and why?

(e) **Tu joues d'un instrument de musique?**

Do you play a musical instrument?

(f) **Tu vas souvent au cinéma?**

Do you often go to the cinema?

(g) **Qu'est-ce que tu aimes faire avec tes copains?**

What do you like to do with your friends?

(h) **Qu'est-ce que tu vas faire le week-end prochain?**

What are you going to do next weekend?

(i) **Qu'est-ce que tu aimes faire à la maison?**

What do you like to do at home?

(j) **Qu'est-ce que tu as fait dimanche dernier?**

What did you do last Sunday?

(k) **Comment est ton week-end idéal?**

What is your ideal weekend like?

Television and cinema

l'acteur (m.)	actor
l'actrice (f.)	actress
le dessin animé	cartoon film
le documentaire	documentary
l'écran (m.)	screen
le feuilleton	soap opera
le film comique	comedy film
le film d'amour	romantic film
le film d'aventures	adventure film
le film d'horreur	horror film
le film de science-fiction	science fiction film
le film policier	detective film
le polar	detective film

le western	western
la chaîne (de télévision)	TV channel
l'émission de sport (f.)	sports programme
la comédie	comedy
la séance	performance, showing (of film)
la série	series
la vedette	star (of stage or film)
les actualités (f.)	news
les informations (f.)	news
avec Gérard Depardieu	starring Gérard Depardieu

Examples:

Je regarde la télé tous les jours.	I watch TV every day.
Mon émission préférée, c'est *Les Simpson*.	My favourite programme is *The Simpsons*.

Exam-style questions

Try these sample exam-style questions for yourself. Suggested answers are given at the back of the book.

Speaking

Role-play practice

Look at the section on the Speaking paper in the Introduction for help with role plays.

Level 2

6.2 You are phoning a friend. Try to say the following in French. The examiner's part is also shown.

(a) Do you want to go to the cinema?

À quelle heure?

(b) There is an adventure film at 3 p.m.

Avec quel acteur?

(c) It's a film with Tom Cruise.

J'adore Tom Cruise.

(d) Let's meet in front of the cinema.

À quelle heure?

(e) Let's meet at 2.30 p.m.

D'accord. Je vais prendre le bus.

(f) Do you want to go to town afterwards?

Non. Mon grand-père vient chez nous ce soir.

Exam-style questions

Try these sample exam-style questions for yourself. Answers are given at the back of the book.

Track 6

Listening

6.3 Listen to this telephone conversation and answer the questions below in English.

- **(a)** When does Marc suggest going to the cinema?
- **(b)** Why does Anne not want to go (two reasons)?
- **(c)** Where do they decide to go next week?
- **(d)** Where will they meet?
- **(e)** Why will they meet here?
- **(f)** At what time will they meet?

Exam-style questions

Try these sample exam-style questions for yourself. Answers are given at the back of the book.

Reading

6.4 Read this interview and answer the questions that follow in English.

Q **Salut, Jean-Marc. Est-ce que tu regardes souvent la télé?**

A Je regarde la télé de temps en temps mais je suis très occupé et je n'ai pas beaucoup de temps libre.

Q **Est-ce que tu as regardé la télé hier soir?**

A Oui. Je n'avais rien à faire hier soir donc j'ai regardé le film *Maman, j'ai raté l'avion* avec ma femme Hélène. Elle aime bien les comédies et c'était très amusant.

Q **Est-ce que tu aimes aller au cinéma?**

A Non, je ne vais jamais au cinéma car il y a trop de monde. Je préfère rester chez moi avec ma famille et mes chiens. D'ailleurs je déteste le popcorn!

Q **Quelle sorte de film est-ce que tu préfères?**

A J'aime bien les comédies comme Hélène mais je préfère les films d'action.

Q **Comment s'appelle ton acteur préféré ou ton actrice préférée?**

A J'adore les films de Gérard Depardieu.

Q **Est-ce que tu as vu les films de Harry Potter?**

A J'ai vu le premier film avec mon fils et j'ai trouvé que c'était amusant mais je me suis endormi pendant le deuxième. Je n'ai pas lu les livres.

Q **Qu'est-ce que ton fils a pensé du film?**

A Patrick a adoré le film et il a lu tous les livres. Il veut être magicien!

Q **Quel est ton film préféré?**

A J'adore *Cyrano de Bergerac*. C'est au sujet d'un homme qui s'appelle Cyrano. Il est laid mais il espère pouvoir un jour séduire son amour de toujours, la belle Roxane, sa cousine. Je l'adore car c'est un film de Gérard Depardieu et c'est une histoire d'amour. Hélène dit que je suis très romantique!

(a) How often does Jean-Marc watch television?

(b) What did he watch on television last night?

(c) Why does he not like to go to the cinema (two reasons)?

(d) What type of film does he prefer?

(e) Who is his favourite actor?

(f) What happened to him during the second Harry Potter film?

(g) What does his son want to be?

(h) How is Cyrano described?

(i) What does Jean-Marc's wife say about Jean-Marc?

6.5 Read the sentences and choose the appropriate picture, as in the example. There are more pictures than you need.

Example:

- *J'adore le cyclisme.*

(a) Je vais envoyer une carte postale à ma tante.

(b) J'adore jouer de la clarinette.

(c) J'ai mal à la tête. Tu as quelque chose?

(d) J'ai soif. Je peux boire un chocolat chaud?

(e) Je vais souvent au cinéma et j'aime bien les comédies.

(f) Mon sport préféré est l'athlétisme.

1

4
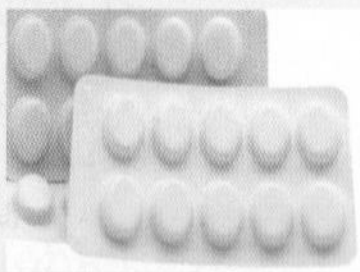

7

2

5

8

3

6

9

6.6 Match up the following types of programmes with the programme titles.

(a) Les informations	1 Match of the Day
(b) Un dessin animé	2 Charlie and Lola
(c) Un documentaire	3 The X Factor
(d) Un drame	4 News at Ten
(e) Une émission de musique	5 Neighbours
(f) Une émission de sport	6 Weather forecast
(g) Une émission pour les petits enfants	7 The Simpsons
(h) La météo	8 Pride and Prejudice
(i) Une série australienne	9 Attenborough and the Giant Elephant

6.7 Read the sentences and choose the appropriate picture, as in the example.

Example:

■ *Je joue d'un instrument de musique.*

(a) Mon frère aime dessiner.

(b) Ma sœur aime jouer au netball.

(c) Maman lit les romans.

(d) Le sport ne m'intéresse pas.

(e) Papa chante.

1

3

5

2

4

Exam-style questions

Try these sample exam-style questions for yourself. Suggested answers are given at the back of the book.

Writing

6.8 Your French friend is coming to stay. Write a list in French of six activities that you could do, as in the example.

(The pictures shown are only a suggestion. You may use any relevant items of vocabulary.)

Example:

- *piano*

6.9 Complete the following sentences by selecting the correct form of the verb or adjective from those given in the brackets.

(a) J'__________ jouer au netball. (aimons, aimez, aime)

(b) Elle __________ dans sa chambre. (dessinez, dessines, dessine)

(c) Est-ce que tu __________ de l'athlétisme? (fais, fait, font)

(d) Son ballon est __________. (bleu, bleue, bleus)

(e) Papa lit une histoire __________. (amusant, amusants, amusante)

6.10 Write a sentence of between five and ten words for each picture.

(a)

(b)

(c)

6.11 Write five short sentences in French about your leisure activities.

Level 2

6.12 Use the vocabulary provided to help you translate the following sentences into French.

(a) I play the piano but my two sisters play the drums.

jouer, piano (m.), sœur (f.), jouer, batterie (f.)

(b) My brother likes to read magazines but I prefer autobiographies.

frère (m.), aimer, lire, magazine (m.), préférer, autobiographie (f.)

(c) My favourite female singer is French.

préféré, chanteuse (f.), français

(d) My uncle is an actor and he likes westerns.

oncle (m.), acteur (m.), aimer, western (m.)

(e) My aunt sings and she loves classical music.

tante (f.), chanter, adorer, classique, musique (f.)

Level 2

6.13 Write an email of between 80 and 120 words to a French friend. You must mention at least four of the following points:

• Un cadeau d'anniversaire	A birthday present
• Une activité avec des amis	An activity with friends
• Un problème	A problem
• Une bonne idée la semaine dernière	A good idea last week
• Un match demain après-midi	A match tomorrow afternoon

★ Make sure you know

★ How to describe both indoor and outdoor activities

★ How to talk about your hobbies and interests

★ How to discuss TV programmes and give your preferences

★ How to talk about music and give your preferences

★ How to describe what you read

★ How to talk about the cinema and films you have seen

Test yourself 28 ✓

Before moving on to the next chapter, make sure you can answer the following questions. Answers, where relevant, are given at the back of the book.

1 Match up the French and English activities.

(a) Je joue avec mes copains.	1 I have to do my homework.
(b) Je regarde les actualités.	2 I want to play on the computer.
(c) J'aime lire des romans.	3 I play with my friends.
(d) Je dois faire mes devoirs.	4 I chat with my friends.
(e) Je veux jouer sur l'ordinateur.	5 I watch TV every evening.
(f) Je voudrais jouer aux cartes.	6 I love cycling.
(g) J'aime lire des BD.	7 I like reading novels.
(h) J'adore faire du vélo.	8 I am watching the news.
(i) Je bavarde avec mes amis.	9 I would like to play cards.
(j) Je regarde la télé tous les soirs.	10 I like reading comics.

2 Copy and complete the following sentences with the correct French verb from the options below.

faire **bavarder** **écouter** **aller** **jouer**

(a) Je n'aime pas ___ en ville.

(b) Elle déteste ___ de la musique.

(c) J'adore ___ au netball.

(d) J'aime ___ du judo.

(e) Il aime ___ avec ses amis.

3 Fill in the following grid with suitable answers in French. Check your answers by looking at the vocabulary lists earlier in the chapter.

	Indoor activities	Outdoor activities	Musical instruments
(a)			
(b)			
(c)			
(d)			
(e)			

7 Life and work at school

The school day

l'anglais (m.)	English	l'éducation religieuse (f.)	religious education
le théâtre (m.)	drama	l'EPS (f.)	PE
le cours	lesson	la géo(graphie)	geography
le français	French	l'histoire (f.)	history
le grec	Greek	l'informatique (f.)	ICT
le latin	Latin	la leçon	lesson
le sport	games	la matière	subject
les maths (f.)	maths	la pause-déjeuner	lunch break
les sciences (f.)	science	la physique	physics
la biologie	biology	la récré(ation)	morning break
la chimie	chemistry	la réunion	assembly
la cuisine	cooking	la technologie	technology

Comments

très bien	very good	difficile	difficult
fantastique	fantastic	dur	hard
intéressant	interesting	ennuyeux	boring
amusant	fun	formidable	great, fantastic
facile	easy		

Dans ma salle de classe il y a ...	In my classroom there is/are ...
le bureau	desk
le sac à dos	rucksack
le tableau blanc	whiteboard
le tableau interactif	interactive board
la chaise	chair
la table	table

À mon école il y a ...	In my school there is/are ...
le bureau	office
le centre sportif	sports centre
le couloir	corridor
le court de tennis	tennis court
le dortoir	dormitory
le gymnase	sports hall
l'internat (m.)	boarding house
le labo(ratoire) de sciences/de langues	science/language lab
le terrain de sport	sports field
la cour	playground
la grande salle	school hall
la piscine	swimming pool
la salle de classe	classroom
la salle d'informatique	computer room
la salle de musique	music room
la salle des professeurs	staff room
les bâtiments (m.)	buildings
les vestiaires (f.)	the changing rooms

Dans mon sac il y a ...	In my bag there is/are ...
l'agenda (m.)	diary
le cahier	exercise book
le compas	compass
le crayon	pencil
le livre	book
le stylo	pen
la calculatrice	calculator
la gomme	eraser
la règle	ruler
la trousse	pencil case

Understanding classroom instructions

lève/levez la main!	put up your hand
lève-toi/levez-vous!	stand up
assieds-toi/asseyez-vous!	sit down
donne-moi ...	give me ...
ouvre la porte, s'il te plaît	open the door, please
ferme la fenêtre	close the window
arrête/arrêtez!	stop
entre/entrez!	come in

*French school children use the word **prof** more frequently than **professeur**, particularly when speaking. The word **professeur** is masculine. If you are specifically talking about a female teacher, you can say **la prof**.

Les gens

l'élève (m. and f.)	pupil
le concierge	male caretaker
la concierge	female caretaker
le directeur	male headteacher
la directrice	female headteacher
l'instituteur (m.)	male primary school teacher
l'institutrice (f.)	female primary school teacher
le prof(esseur)*	teacher
sévère	strict
strict	strict
gentil, gentille	kind

Verbs

commencer	to begin	passer un examen	to sit an exam
compter	to count	réussir	to succeed
emprunter	to borrow	réussir à un examen	to pass an exam
faire les devoirs	to do homework		

Useful phrases

Je suis en cinquième	I am in Year 8
Je suis externe	I am a day pupil
Je suis interne	I am a boarder
Je suis demi-pensionnaire	I am a half-boarder (eat lunch at school)
Je suis faible en biologie	I am weak at biology
Je suis fort(e) en histoire	I am good at history
Ça s'écrit comment?	How do you spell that?
Excusez-moi	Excuse me
Je ne sais pas	I do not know
Ma matière préférée est …	My favourite subject is …
Chaque cours dure 45 minutes	Each lesson lasts 45 minutes
J'ai oublié	I have forgotten
Deux fois par semaine	Twice a week
Je n'ai pas de stylo	I do not have a pen
J'ai perdu …	I have lost …

Test your speaking

Read the sample passages aloud then say a few sentences about your school in the same way.

Salut! Je m'appelle Jack et je vais à une école privée dans le sud de l'Angleterre. Il y a 300 élèves à l'école et elle se trouve à la campagne. Ma matière préférée est l'histoire car c'est intéressant et le professeur est assez strict mais patient.

Bonjour, je m'appelle Patricia et je vais au collège à Édimbourg. J'adore mon collège car je suis sportive et il y a beaucoup de choses à faire. Il y a des terrains de sport, des courts de tennis et un centre sportif. L'année prochaine ils vont construire une piscine couverte. C'est formidable!

Je vais à l'école à pied parce qu'il y a trop de circulation. Je quitte la maison à sept heures quarante-cinq et j'entre dans ma salle de classe à huit heures cinq. Les cours commencent à neuf heures moins le quart après la réunion.

Exam-style questions

Try these sample exam-style questions for yourself. Suggested answers are given at the back of the book.

Speaking

Oral discussions

7.1 **(a)** Décris une journée typique à l'école.

Describe a typical day at school.

(b) Combien de cours as-tu par jour?

How many lessons do you have each day?

(c) Les devoirs durent combien de temps?

How long does your homework take?

(d) Quelles matières aimes-tu?

Which subjects do you like?

(e) Fais-moi une description de ton école.

Describe your school.

(f) Est-ce que tu aimes ton école? Pourquoi (pas)?

Do you like your school? Why (not)?

(g) Qu'est-ce que tu fais pendant la récréation?

What can you do during break?

(h) Qu'est-ce que tu aimes faire à l'école quand tu n'as pas de cours?

What do you like to do at school when you do not have any lessons?

(i) Qu'est-ce que tu vas faire cet après-midi?

What are you going to do this afternoon?

(j) Qu'est-ce que tu as fait hier à l'école?

What did you do yesterday at school?

(k) Qu'est-ce que tu portes comme uniforme scolaire?

What do you wear as school uniform?

Role-play practice

Look at the section on the Speaking paper in the Introduction for help with role plays.

Level 2

7.2 You are at school in France with your penfriend. Try to say the following in French. The examiner's part is also shown.

(a) I do not have a pen.

Voici un stylo.

(b) Do you have a ruler?

Non, je n'ai pas de règle.

(c) What is the date?

C'est le cinq mars. Tu comprends le professeur?

(d) The teacher speaks too fast.

Mais il est gentil.

(e) At what time does the lesson end?

À dix heures vingt.

(f) The lessons are very long in France.

Oui. Malheureusement!

Level 2

7.3 You are at school in France with your penfriend. Try to say the following in French. The examiner's part is also shown.

(a) The school is very big.

Oui. C'est vrai.

(b) How many pupils are there?

Il y a quatre cents élèves.

(c) My school is smaller.

Il y a combien d'élèves à ton école?

(d) There are 80 boys and 55 girls.

C'est petit.

(e) At what time does the first lesson begin?

À neuf heures.

(f) Lessons begin at 8.30 a.m. in my school.

C'est tôt.

Level 2

7.4 You are at school in France and are talking to the teacher. Try to say the following in French. The examiner's part is also shown.

(a) Can I come in?

Oui. Bien sûr.

(b) I am staying with my penfriend.

Quel âge as-tu?

(c) I am 13 years old.

Tu es en vacances?

(d) I am here for one week.

Bienvenue à notre école.

(e) Do I have to do homework?

Oui, comme les autres élèves.

(f) I do homework every day in England.

C'est une bonne idée.

Exam-style questions

Try these sample exam-style questions for yourself. Answers are given at the back of the book.

Track 7

Listening

7.5 Listen to Julie describe her school. For each sentence, choose the correct picture.

Example:

Je me lève à sept heures.

I get up at ___________.

Picture 1

1

2

3

(a) I go to school ______.

1

2

3

(b) I arrive at school at ______.

1

2

3

(c) My favourite subject is ______.

1

2

3

(d) On Wednesday afternoon we have a ____ match.

1

2

3

(e) This evening I have to ____.

1

2

3

Track 8

7.6 Listen to the boy talking about his school and choose the correct answer, as in the example.

Example:

Mon école se trouve à Bordeaux.

My school is in *Bordeaux.*

Manchester London ~~Bordeaux~~

(a) It is a school for ____.	boys	girls	boys and girls
(b) There are ____ pupils.	100	170	160
(c) His favourite subject is ____.	PE	biology	physics
(d) The teacher has ____.	long curly hair	short curly hair	short straight hair
(e) He likes ____.	art	drama	maths

Track 9

7.7 Listen to this boy and choose a picture for each thing he says, as in the example.

Example:

J'adore jouer de la trompette.

Picture 1

1

3

5

2

4

6

Exam-style questions

Try these sample exam-style questions for yourself. Answers are given at the back of the book.

Reading

7.8 Read the following text and indicate whether the statements are TRUE or FALSE by ticking the correct box, as in the example.

Jean-Paul a treize ans et il est en cinquième. Il va à une école privée dans le sud-ouest de l'Angleterre. C'est une école mixte à la campagne et il y a environ 180 élèves. Sa matière préférée, c'est le dessin mais il aime aussi l'histoire et le latin. Il fait ses devoirs cinq fois par semaine et le week-end il fait du sport. Il aime bien la natation et il y a une piscine à son école.

	TRUE	FALSE
Example: Jean-Paul is 13 years old.	✓	
(a) His school is in the south-east of England.		
(b) There are 180 pupils in his school.		
(c) He does not like Latin.		
(d) He does homework five times a week.		
(e) He really likes swimming.		

7.9 Read the following passage, then copy and complete it by filling in the gaps using the words below. Each word can only be used once.

patient clubs mixte sportif élèves dure heures commencent échecs treize bibliothèque expériences test

Mon école s'appelle Brockett Hall. C'est une école privée et ____. Il y a environ deux cents ____ de huit à ____ ans et douze professeurs. Mon école est bien équipée. Par exemple, il y a un nouveau gymnase et la ____ a été construite il y a dix-huit mois. Je ne suis pas très ____ mais j'adore la lecture.

J'arrive à l'école à huit ____ vingt et les cours ____ quinze minutes plus tard. Il y a une récré à onze heures moins cinq et ça ____ vingt-cinq minutes. Il y a beaucoup de ____ pendant la pause-déjeuner. Pour les élèves qui aiment les sports, il y a des clubs comme le rugby et le netball mais, moi, j'aime jouer aux ____.

Ma matière préférée, c'est l'histoire et je m'intéresse beaucoup à la Deuxième Guerre mondiale. J'ai horreur des sciences parce que le professeur n'est pas ____. Je trouve les ____ fatigantes et nous avons fait un ____ hier matin.

Exam-style questions

Try these sample exam-style questions for yourself. Suggested answers are given at the back of the book.

Writing

7.10 Your French friend is coming to your school. Write a list in French of six things in your classroom, as in the example.

(The pictures shown are only a suggestion. You may use any relevant items of vocabulary.)

Example:

■ *crayons*

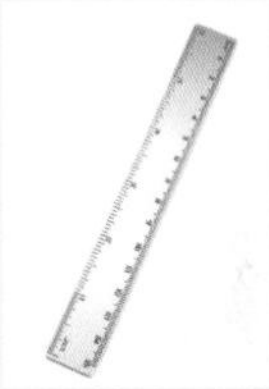

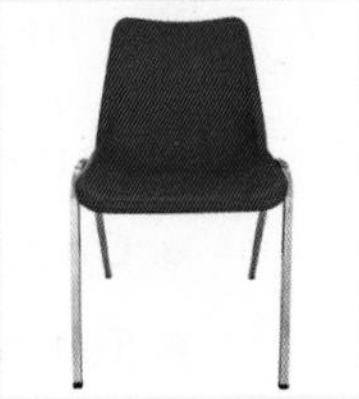

7.11 Complete the following sentences by selecting the correct form of the verb or adjective from those given in the brackets.

(a) Je ______ jouer sur l'ordinateur. (veut, voulez, veux)

(b) Anne-Marie ______ avec ses amies dans la salle de classe. (bavardez, bavardons, bavarde)

(c) Il ______ l'histoire car le prof est très strict. (détestons, déteste, détestes)

(d) ______ la fenêtre, s'il te plaît, Henri. (Ferme, Fermes, Fermez)

(e) Les chaises dans ma salle de classe sont ______. (bleus, bleue, bleues)

7.12 Write a sentence of between five and ten words for each picture.

(a)

(b)

7.13 Write five short sentences in French about your school subjects.

Level 2

7.14 Use the vocabulary provided to help you translate the following sentences into French.

(a) The lessons begin at nine o'clock.

cours (m.), commencer, heure (f.)

(b) I prefer maths because the teacher is funny.

préférer, maths (f.), professeur (m.), amusant

(c) My friends are boarders but I am a day pupil.

ami (m.), interne (m.), externe (m.)

(d) The headteacher is very strict but he is also quite sporty.

directeur (m.), strict, sportif

(e) I love to play netball and my mother likes to watch the matches.

adorer, jouer, netball (m.), mère (f.), aimer, regarder, match (m.)

Level 2

7.15 Your French friend is coming to visit you and has asked you to send a brief description of life in an English school. Write an email of 80–120 words. You must mention at least four of the following points:

• Où se trouve ton école	Where your school is
• Tes matières préférées	Your favourite subjects
• Le sport et les activités	Sport and activities
• Les cours d'hier	Yesterday's lessons
• Les activités de demain	Tomorrow's activities

L'informatique	Computing
cliquer sur …	to click on …
effacer	to delete
entrer	to enter, log on
répondre	to reply
sauvegarder	to save
sortir	to go out, log off
surfer sur Internet	to surf the internet
télécharger	to download
le clavier	keyboard
le courriel	email
le courrier électronique	email (service, system)
le document	document

L'informatique	Computing
le dossier	file
l'écran (m.)	screen
l'e-mail (m.)	email
Internet (m.)	the internet
le mot de passe	password
l'ordinateur (m.)	computer
le site Internet/Web	website
l'imprimante (f.)	printer
la souris	mouse

★ Make sure you know

- ★ How to describe your school
- ★ How to describe the people in your school
- ★ How to talk about your school day
- ★ How to talk about school subjects
- ★ How to discuss what you like and dislike at school
- ★ How to understand classroom instructions
- ★ How to understand computer terminology

Test yourself 29 ✓

Before moving on to the next chapter, make sure you can answer the following questions. Answers, where relevant, are given at the back of the book.

1 Read the descriptions of what happens in each room (on the left) and choose the correct classroom (on the right).

Dans cette salle on étudie …

(a)	la langue et la littérature de la Grande Bretagne.	1	la salle de musique
(b)	la biologie, la chimie et la physique.	2	la salle d'anglais
(c)	des mélodies ou des chansons.	3	la salle de géographie
(d)	les gens célèbres et les dates dans le passé.	4	la salle d'histoire
(e)	les rivières, la campagne et la météo.	5	le labo

2 Write down ten things that you would find in a classroom. Check the vocabulary lists in this chapter for your spellings.

8 Holidays, weather, time and dates

8.1 Weather, time and dates

Seasons

en automne	in autumn	au printemps	in spring
en hiver	in winter	en été	in summer

Weather adjectives

* Note that these are used with the verb faire.

For example: il fait chaud (it is hot).

agréable	pleasant	froid*	cold
beau*	lovely, fine	humide	humid
brumeux	misty	mauvais*	bad
chaud*	hot	nuageux	cloudy
clair	clear	orageux	stormy
couvert	overcast	pluvieux	rainy
doux*	mild	sec	dry
frais	fresh	variable	variable

Examples:

Il fait doux aujourd'hui.	It is mild today.
Il a fait chaud hier.	It was hot yesterday.
Le temps était agréable.	The weather was pleasant.
Le ciel est couvert.	The sky is overcast.

Weather nouns

l'arc-en-ciel (m.)	rainbow	le verglas	black ice
le ciel	sky	la brume	mist
un coup de tonnerre	a clap of thunder	la chaleur	heat
un coup de vent	a gust of wind	des éclaircies (f.)	sunny spells
un éclair (m.)	a flash of lightning	la glace	ice
un orage	a storm	la grêle	hail
le soleil	sun	la neige	snow
le tonnerre	thunder	la pluie	rain
le vent	wind	une tempête	a storm

Weather phrases

Quel temps fait-il?	What is the weather like?
Il fait 30 degrés	It is 30 degrees
Il fait de la grêle	It is hailing
Il y a du brouillard	It is foggy
Il gèle	It is freezing
Il neige	It is snowing
Il pleut	It is raining
Il fait du tonnerre	It is thundering
Le soleil brille	The sun is shining
Il faisait beau	It was good weather
Il y avait de l'orage	It was stormy
Il neigeait	It was snowing
Il pleuvait	It was raining
Le soleil brillait	The sun was shining

Time nouns

le coucher du soleil	sunset	toute la journée	the whole day
le lever du soleil	sunrise	le soir	evening
l'aube (f.)	dawn	la soirée	evening (all evening)
le jour	day	le mois	month
quinze jours	a fortnight	le siècle	century
la journée	day (whole day long)		

Examples:

J'ai passé quinze jours en Écosse.	I spent a fortnight in Scotland.
Elle a passé la soirée devant la télé.	She spent the evening in front of the TV.
Bonne journée!	Have a good day!
Bonne soirée!	Enjoy your evening!

When?

aujourd'hui	today
ce matin	this morning
cet après-midi	this afternoon
ce soir	this evening
hier	yesterday
hier soir	yesterday evening/last night
avant-hier	the day before yesterday
la veille	the previous day
le week-end dernier	last weekend
la semaine dernière	last week
il y a trois mois	three months ago

pendant les vacances	in/during the holidays
demain	tomorrow
demain matin	tomorrow morning
après-demain	the day after tomorrow
le lendemain	the next day
l'an prochain (m.)	next year
dimanche prochain	next Sunday
la semaine prochaine	next week
à l'avenir	in the future
le premier avril	(on) the 1st of April
le deux février	(on) the 2nd of February

Special days

un jour férié	a bank holiday
un jour de fête	a day of celebration
l'anniversaire (f.)	birthday
une fête	a party
fêter	to celebrate
une fête religieuse	a religious festival
la Fête des Mères	Mothers' Day
la Fête des Pères	Fathers' Day
le Mardi Gras	Shrove Tuesday
le jour de l'An	New Year's Day
Noël	Christmas
Pâques	Easter
l'Aïd (f.)	Eid
Diwali	Diwali
la Hanoukka	Hanukkah
le 14 juillet/la Fête Nationale	Bastille Day

Greetings

Bon anniversaire!	Happy birthday!
Bonne fête!	Enjoy your special day!
Joyeux Noël!	Happy Christmas!
Joyeuses Pâques!	Happy Easter!
Bonne année!	Happy New Year!
Bonnes vacances!	Have a good holiday!

Time and date phrases

Quelle heure est-il?	What time is it?
Il est trois heures	It is three o'clock
Il est trois heures cinq	It is five past three
Il est trois heures moins cinq	It is five to three
Il est trois heures et quart	It is quarter past three
Il est trois heures et demie	It is half past three
Il est trois heures moins le quart	It is quarter to three
Ça commence à quelle heure?	At what time does it begin?
À dix-huit heures	At 18.00
À minuit et demi	At half past 12 (midnight)
À midi et demi	At half past 12 (noon)
Quelle est la date aujourd'hui?	What is the date today?
C'est quand?	When is it?
C'est quand ton anniversaire?	When is your birthday?
C'est le cinq avril	It is the 5th of April
Tu es en avance	You are early
Tu es en retard	You are late
À tout à l'heure	See you soon
À ce soir	See you this evening
À bientôt	See you soon
Il se fait tard	It is getting late

? Exam-style questions

Try these sample exam-style questions for yourself. Suggested answers are given at the back of the book.

Speaking

Role-play practice

Look at the section on the Speaking paper in the Introduction for help with role plays.

Level 2

8.1 You are on the phone to a French penfriend. Try to say the following in French. The examiner's part is also shown.

(a) What is the weather like there?

Il fait très beau aujourd'hui. Et chez toi?

(b) It is warm here, but it is raining.

Quel dommage.

(c) When is your birthday?

Mon anniversaire, c'est le dix-neuf mai.

(d) What are you going to do at Christmas?

Je vais en Espagne avec ma famille.

(e) I love to go skiing in winter.

Moi, je n'aime pas faire du ski. J'aime faire des randonnées.

(f) Goodbye.

À bientôt.

Exam-style questions

Try these sample exam-style questions for yourself. Answers are given at the back of the book.

Reading

8.2 Pick the phrases that describe fine weather from the list below.

(a) Il fait beau

(b) Il neige

(c) Il ne fait pas chaud

(d) Il y a du brouillard

(e) Il gèle

(f) Il fait de l'orage

(g) Il fait mauvais

(h) Il pleut

(i) Il fait 30 degrés

8.3 Read the following advert and fill in the gaps in the questions that follow.

PISCINE EN PLEIN AIR

Heures d'ouverture

Du lundi au vendredi:	de 10h à 12h30 de 14h à 17h
Le week-end:	de 9h à 12h30 de 13h à 20h

TARIF

Entrée: **4 euros**

Enfants 5 à 13 ans: **3 euros**

Les moins de 5 ans: **gratuit**

Example:

L'information est pour *la piscine*.

1 **l'église**

2 **le cinéma**

3 **la piscine** ✓

(a) La piscine ouvre à ______ le lundi.

1 9 heures
2 10 heures
3 11 heures

(b) La piscine ferme à ______ le dimanche.

1 6 heures
2 20 heures
3 10 heures

(c) Un garçon qui a treize ans paie ______.

1 4 euros
2 3 euros
3 0 euros

(d) Une fille qui a quatre ans paie ______.

1 4 euros
2 3 euros
3 0 euros

(e) Un adulte paie ______.

1 4 euros
2 3 euros
3 0 euros

8.4 Choose the correct sentence from the options below for each picture, as in the example.

Example:

■ *Il est neuf heures.*

~~**Il est neuf heures.**~~
Il est neuf heures moins le quart.
Il est neuf heures et demie.
Il est neuf heures et quart.
Il est neuf heures cinq.
Il est neuf heures vingt.

(a) 

(c) 

(e) 

(b) 

(d) 

Exam-style questions

Try these sample exam-style questions for yourself. Suggested answers are given at the back of the book.

Writing

8.5 Your French friend asks what the weather is like where you live. Write a list in French of six weather words, as in the example.

(The pictures shown are only a suggestion. You may use any relevant items of vocabulary.)

Example:

■ *soleil*

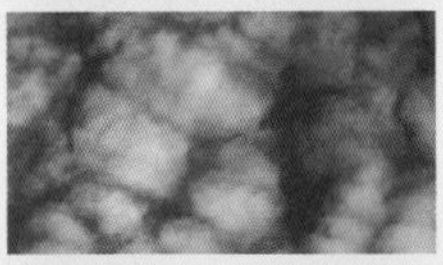

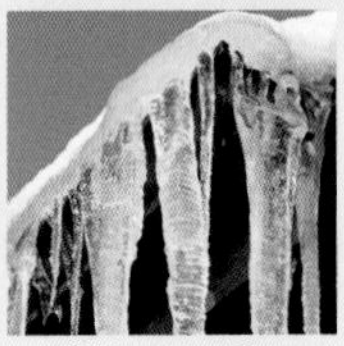

8.6 Complete the following sentences by selecting the correct form of the verb or adjective from those given in the brackets.

(a) Il _____ beau aujourd'hui. (fais, fait, font)

(b) Il _____ trois heures trente. (es, est, êtes)

(c) Tu _____ en retard. (es, est, sommes)

(d) Marc va partir la semaine _____. (prochain, prochaine, prochains)

(e) Le ciel est _____. (couvert, couverte, couverts)

8.7 Write five short sentences in French about your favourite festival or festivals.

8.2 Describing holidays and holiday activities

Places to stay

l'hôtel (m.)	hotel	l'auberge (f.)	inn, small hotel
le gîte	rented cottage	le camping	campsite

At the hotel

le sèche-cheveux	hairdryer	la pension complète	full board
les bagages (m.)	luggage	la serviette	towel
la clef/la clé	key	la valise	suitcase
la demi-pension	half board	la vue sur la mer	sea view

Useful phrases

C'est ...	It is ...
au sous-sol	in the basement
au rez-de-chaussée	on the ground floor
au premier étage	on the first floor
au deuxième étage	on the second floor
au dessus de ...	above ...
au dessous de ...	below ...

At the campsite

le bloc sanitaire	wash block	le sac de couchage	sleeping bag
le camping-car	motorhome	l'allumette (f.)	match
l'emplacement (m.)	pitch	la douche	shower
le feu	fire	l'eau non potable (f.)	non-drinking water
le gaz	gas	la lampe de poche	torch
le matelas pneumatique	airbed	la pile	battery
l'ouvre-boîte (m.)	can opener	la tente	tent
des plats à emporter	takeaway meals		

Examples:

Est-ce que vous avez de la place?

Do you have any vacancies?

Est-ce que vous avez des chambres libres?

Do you have any rooms free?

À quel étage est la chambre?

On which floor is the bedroom?

Avez-vous de la place pour une tente pour quatre nuits?

Do you have space for a tent for four nights?

Je voudrais réserver un emplacement pour quatre personnes et une tente.

I would like to reserve a pitch for four people and a tent.

At the seaside

le bateau	boat	la crème solaire	suncream
le marchand de glaces	ice cream vendor	la falaise	cliff
le phare	lighthouse	la marée (basse/haute)	(low/high) tide
le rocher	rock	la mer	sea
le sable	sand	faire un barbecue	to have a barbecue
		faire un pique-nique	to have a picnic

Countries and nationalities

l'Allemagne (f.)	Germany	allemand(e)	German
les États-Unis (m.)	USA	américain(e)	American
l'Angleterre (f.)	England	anglais(e)	English
la Belgique	Belgium	belge	Belgian
le Canada	Canada	canadien(ne)	Canadian
l'Écosse (f.)	Scotland	écossais(e)	Scottish
l'Espagne (f.)	Spain	espagnol(e)	Spanish
la France	France	français(e)	French
la Grande-Bretagne	Great Britain	britannique	British
l'Irlande (f.)	Ireland	irlandais(e)	Irish
les Pays-Bas (m.)	Netherlands	néerlandais(e)	Dutch
le pays de Galles	Wales	gallois(e)	Welsh
la Suisse	Switzerland	suisse	Swiss

Useful phrases

Je suis en vacances	I am on holiday
Pendant les grandes vacances	During the summer holidays
Je suis allé(e) à Londres	I went to London
J'ai voyagé en voiture	I travelled by car
Je suis resté(e) à la maison	I stayed at home
J'ai passé une semaine en Écosse	I spent a week in Scotland
Je suis allé(e) à l'étranger	I went abroad

Positive opinions

J'ai aimé mon séjour parce que/qu' ...	I liked my stay because ...
c'était intéressant	it was interesting
il faisait beau	there was good weather
j'ai fait beaucoup de choses	I did a lot of things
l'hôtel était énorme	the hotel was enormous
il y avait une piscine en plein air	there was an outdoor swimming pool
la nourriture était délicieuse	the food was delicious

Negative opinions

Je n'ai pas aimé mon séjour parce que/qu' ...	I did not like my stay because ...
c'était ennuyeux	it was boring
il faisait froid	it was cold
il faisait trop chaud	it was too hot
j'ai visité trop de musées	I visited too many museums
il n'y avait pas de piscine	there was no swimming pool
l'hôtel était petit	the hotel was small

Test your speaking ✓

Read the following three passages aloud and note that each passage is in a different tense: the first is in the **present tense** as the person is saying what they **normally** do; the second is in the **past**, talking about a holiday they have **spent** in Biarritz; the third is telling what they are **going** to be doing next year.

Pendant les grandes vacances nous passons normalement une semaine au bord de la mer. J'adore aller à la plage. Je nage et je joue au foot avec mes frères.

J'ai aimé mon séjour à Biarritz parce que l'hôtel était énorme avec une piscine magnifique et un très bon restaurant. Aussi, l'hôtel était à cent mètres de la plage. Le dernier jour j'ai nagé dans la mer avant le petit-déjeuner et, après avoir mangé, je suis allé en ville acheter des cadeaux pour mes amis.

L'année prochaine je vais aller au Canada. Ça va être formidable! Nous allons rester chez mes cousins qui habitent à Vancouver. Je vais faire du kayak et de la voile et nous allons faire des randonnées dans la forêt.

Now make up a few sentences in the same way on the subject of your holidays.

? Exam-style questions

Try these sample exam-style questions for yourself. Suggested answers are given at the back of the book.

Speaking

Oral discussions

8.8 **(a)** **Qu'est-ce que tu aimes faire pendant les grandes vacances?**

What do you like to do during the summer holidays?

(b) **Décris une journée typique pendant les vacances.**

Describe a typical day during the holidays.

(c) **Qu'est-ce que tu aimes faire quand il fait chaud?**

What do you like to do when it is hot?

(d) **Où es-tu allé(e) en vacances l'année dernière?**

Where did you go on holiday last year?

(e) **Décris-moi un peu ces vacances.**

Tell me a little about this holiday.

Role-play practice

Look at the section on the Speaking paper in the Introduction for help with role plays.

Level 2

8.9 You are on the beach and meet a French child. Try to say the following in French. The examiner's part is also shown.

(a) Hello. My name is John.

Bonjour, John.

(b) It is very hot today.

Oui, c'est vrai.

(c) Where do you live?

J'habite à cinq minutes d'ici.

(d) Is the weather always good?

Oui. Tu es en vacances?

(e) Yes. I am here for two weeks.

C'est ta première fois ici?

(f) I spend my holidays here every year.

Bonnes vacances!

Level 2

8.10 You are at a campsite. Try to say the following in French. The examiner's part is also shown.

(a) I would like a pitch, please.

Vous avez combien de tentes?

(b) We have one tent.

Il y a combien de personnes dans votre famille?

(c) There are five people in my family.

Vous voulez rester combien de nuits?

(d) We want to stay for four nights.

Pas de problème.

(e) Where is the wash block?

C'est là-bas, à gauche.

(f) Is there a swimming pool?

Oui, c'est derrière le parking.

Level 2

8.11 You are at a hotel. Try to say the following in French. The examiner's part is also shown.

(a) Do you have any free rooms?

C'est pour combien de personnes?

(b) It is for two adults and three children.

Pas de problème.

(c) How much is it?

C'est 30 euros par personne.

(d) Is there a shower in the room?

Oui, il y a une douche.

(e) Can we eat in the hotel now?

Malheureusement, le restaurant est fermé.

(f) Is there a restaurant nearby?

Oui, il y a un petit restaurant au bout de la rue.

Exam-style questions

Try these sample exam-style questions for yourself. Answers are given at the back of the book.

Listening

Track 10

8.12 Match each description you hear with the correct event below.

1 Le jour de l'An
2 L'Armistice 1918
3 La Fête Nationale
4 Pâques

Exam-style questions

Try these sample exam-style questions for yourself. Answers are given at the back of the book.

Reading

8.13 Read the following passage and answer the questions that follow in English.

Cette année nous avons passé une semaine dans un petit camping au bord de la mer. Nous avons loué une tente parce que, l'année dernière, on a eu un accident avec notre tente quand il faisait trop de vent. J'ai monté la tente avec Papa pendant l'après-midi et Maman est allée au magasin avec mes deux petites sœurs. Il faisait très chaud donc Maman a acheté des glaces pour tout le monde et nous nous sommes assis sous un arbre. C'était un grand emplacement donc il y avait beaucoup d'espace pour notre voiture et les cinq vélos.

J'étais un peu fatigué, alors j'ai cherché un matelas pneumatique et je me suis reposé pendant un quart d'heure pendant que Papa finissait tout. Après dix minutes il a décidé d'aller au café pour acheter des plats à emporter. Il voulait préparer un barbecue mais c'était interdit parce que l'emplacement se trouvait à côté d'un bois.

(a) How long did they spend on holiday?

(b) What happened last year?

(c) How many people are there in the family?

(d) What did Mum buy?

(e) Why is a mattress mentioned?

(f) What did Dad want to do?

(g) Why could he not do it?

8.14 Read the following passage and answer the questions that follow in English.

La tour Eiffel a été construite en 1889 pour L'Exposition Universelle de Paris, qui a célébré le centenaire de la Révolution française. Il y avait un concours et les plans de Monsieur Gustave Eiffel ont été choisis. Après deux ans, on a fini la construction et la tour Eiffel est restée l'édifice le plus haut du monde jusqu'en 1930. Elle mesure trois cents mètres et il y a trois niveaux. Il y a eu une pétition signée pour protester contre sa construction mais, actuellement, c'est une des attractions les plus célèbres du monde entier. Il y a un restaurant, un bar et une boutique. La tour est aussi très utile avec ses antennes pour la radio et la télévision françaises.

(a) When was the Eiffel Tower built?

(b) Why was the Eiffel Tower built?

(c) How many metres tall is the Eiffel Tower?

(d) Why was a petition signed?

(e) Why is the Eiffel Tower useful?

Exam-style questions

Try these sample exam-style questions for yourself. Suggested answers are given at the back of the book.

Writing

8.15 Write a sentence of between five and ten words for each picture.

(a) 

(b) 

Level 2

8.16 Use the vocabulary provided to help you translate the following sentences into French.

(a) The sun is shining and I am watching television.

soleil (m.), briller, regarder, télévision (f.)

(b) It is my mother's birthday and my father is making a cake.

mère (f.), anniversaire (m.), père (m.), faire, gâteau (m.)

(c) It is nine o'clock and I am going to buy a newspaper.

heure (f.), aller, acheter, journal (m.)

(d) I am in a big hotel and there is a beautiful sea view.

grand, hôtel (m.), beau, vue (f.), mer (f.)

(e) There are four showers and 30 tents at the campsite.

douche (f.), camping (m.), tente (f.)

Level 2

8.17 You are writing to a French friend about a special day. Write an email of 80–120 words. You must mention at least four of the following points:

- Le départ en bus — Departure by bus
- Les activités à la plage — Activities at the beach
- Le repas en ville — The meal in town
- Les activités du soir — Activities in the evening
- Demain matin — Tomorrow morning

8.18 You are spending a week at a seaside resort and each day you fill in your diary. You can mention the weather, where you have been, what you have been doing, who you have met, what you have eaten, etc. Write five to ten words for each daily entry.

Lundi:
Mardi:
Mercredi:
Jeudi:
Vendredi:
Samedi:
Dimanche:

★ Make sure you know

- ★ How to discuss the weather
- ★ How to talk about special days and events
- ★ How to discuss where you can stay on holiday
- ★ How to describe where you have been on holiday
- ★ How to talk about future holiday plans

Test yourself 30 ✓

Before moving on to the next chapter, make sure you can answer the following questions. Answers, where relevant, are given at the back of the book.

1 How many types of weather can you say in French? Try to write them down and check your spellings from the lists in this chapter.

2 Do you know the French for Christmas, New Year, Easter, Shrove Tuesday, Bastille Day and any other festivals that are important to you?

3 C'était comment?

Work out which of these opinions are positive and which are negative:

génial bizarre excellent bruyant extra super bien trop long formidable bon marché nul incroyable trop court intéressant trop cher désastreux fantastique chouette affreux ennuyeux tranquille stressant confortable cool

4 Which of these activities are often done on the beach?

(a) Je mange une glace au chocolat.

(b) Je joue avec un ballon.

(c) Je fais du shopping.

(d) Je fais mes devoirs.

(e) Je passe l'aspirateur.

(f) Je me bronze.

9 Health and fitness

Parts of the body

le bras	arm	la dent	tooth
le dos	back	l'épaule (f.)	shoulder
le genou	knee	la gorge	throat
le nez	nose	la jambe	leg
l'œil (m.)	eye	la main	hand
le pied	foot	l'oreille (f.)	ear
le ventre	stomach	la tête	head
les yeux	eyes		

Qu'est-ce qui ne va pas?	What is the matter?
J'ai mal à la tête	I have a headache
J'ai mal à l'oreille	I have earache
J'ai mal au dos	I have a sore back
J'ai mal aux yeux	My eyes hurt

Health

le comprimé	tablet, pill	un rhume	a cold
un coup de soleil	sunstroke	le sparadrap	sticking plaster
l'infirmier (m.)	male nurse	le tube de crème solaire	tube of suncream
le médecin	doctor		
le médicament	medicine	l'aspirine (f.)	aspirin
le pansement	dressing, bandage	la grippe	flu
le paracétamol	paracetamol	l'infirmière (f.)	female nurse
le pharmacien	chemist	la maladie	illness
		la pharmacie	chemist's

Verbs

avoir besoin de	to need	fumer	to smoke
avoir chaud	to feel hot	grossir	to put on weight
avoir faim	to be hungry	maigrir	to lose weight
avoir froid	to feel cold	mourir	to die
avoir le mal de mer	to be seasick	prendre rendez-vous	to make an appointment
avoir soif	to be thirsty	prendre un coup de soleil	to get sunstroke
casser	to break	se blesser	to injure oneself
être en forme	to be fit	se faire mal	to hurt oneself
être malade	to be ill	vomir	to vomit

Useful phrases

j'ai froid	I am cold
j'ai chaud	I am hot
je suis malade	I am ill
ça ne va pas	I am not well
je dois rester au lit	I must stay in bed
je suis enrhumé(e)	I have a cold
je me suis cassé la jambe	I have broken my leg
elle va téléphoner au médecin*	she is going to phone the doctor
bonjour, Docteur*	good morning, Doctor

*Note that the normal word for 'doctor' is médecin but you address him/her as Docteur.

Test your writing ✓

Write an email to a French friend explaining that you are at home today because you are unwell. Explain what the problem is, whether you have been to the doctor, how you are feeling now and what you are planning to do tomorrow.

? Exam-style questions

Try these sample exam-style questions for yourself. Suggested answers are given at the back of the book.

Speaking

Role-play practice
Look at the section on the Speaking paper in the Introduction for help with role plays.

Level 2

9.1 You are at the chemist's. Try to say the following in French. The examiner's part is also shown.

(a) I am ill.

Qu'est-ce que vous avez?

(b) I have a headache.

Vous êtes enrhumé(e)?

(c) I am very hot.

Vous voulez acheter des paracétamols?

(d) Yes. Can I telephone the doctor?

Oui, vous pouvez téléphoner de chez vous.

(e) I am staying with my French friend.

Alors, vous pouvez téléphoner de chez votre ami(e).

(f) What is the doctor called?

Duroc.

Level 2

9.2 You are at the doctor's. Try to say the following in French. The examiner's part is also shown.

(a) I have earache.

Avez-vous d'autres problèmes?

(b) I am not able to sleep.

Est-ce que vous voulez manger?

(c) I am not hungry.

Je vois le problème. Voici une ordonnance.

(d) Where is the chemist's?

C'est sur la route, à côté de l'église.

(e) Is the chemist's open today?

Oui, jusqu'à cinq heures.

(f) Can I have paracetamol?

Oui, bien sûr.

Exam-style questions

Try these sample exam-style questions for yourself. Answers are given at the back of the book.

Reading

9.3 Read these problems and match the name of each person to one of the statements that follow.

Je dois porter des lunettes mais je ne veux pas les porter parce que les autres élèves dans ma classe se moquent de moi. Je ne peux pas bien voir si je ne les porte pas et j'ai mal à la tête. *Anne*

Tous les matins je me lave soigneusement mais je suis adolescent et des boutons se sont formés sur tout mon visage. Qu'est-ce que je peux faire? *Paul*

J'ai voulu changer la couleur de mes cheveux mais, la semaine dernière, j'ai commencé à perdre mes cheveux. Je ne veux pas me cacher de mes amis donc qu'est-ce que je peux faire? *Martine*

J'adore aller à la plage avec mes copines. Nous jouons au volley et j'adore me bronzer. Est-ce que le bronzage présente des dangers? *Cathérine*

Mon frère est très sportif et il joue toujours au basket avec ses amis. Il dit que je dois y jouer aussi mais je ne suis pas en forme et je suis assez gros. Je veux maigrir mais je ne sais pas comment. *Marc*

(a) I worry about sunbathing.

(b) I want to get thinner.

(c) I do not want to wear my glasses.

(d) I'm worried about my hair starting to fall out.

(e) I would like advice about my spots.

Exam-style questions

Try these sample exam-style questions for yourself. Suggested answers are given at the back of the book.

Writing

9.4 You are at the doctor's in France. Write a list in French of six parts of the body, as in the example.

(The pictures shown are only a suggestion. You may use any relevant items of vocabulary.)

Example:

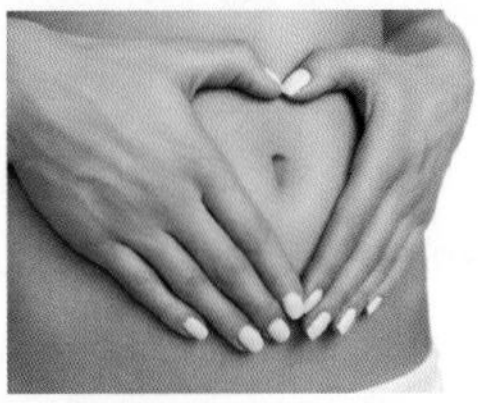

■ *ventre*

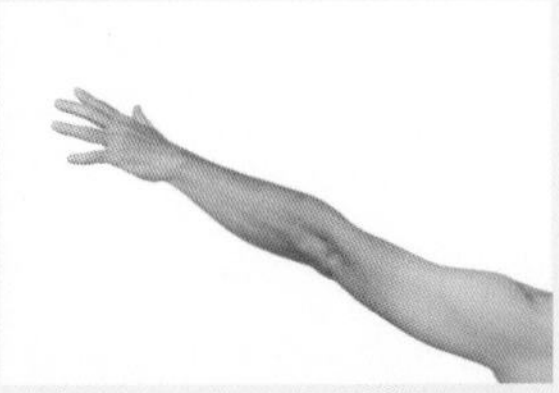

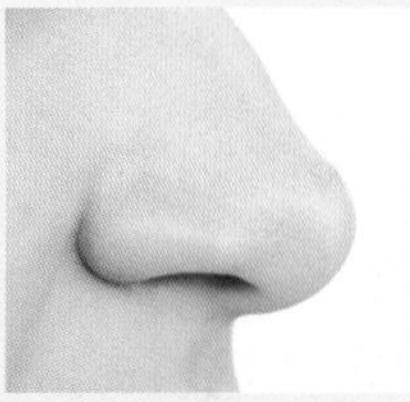

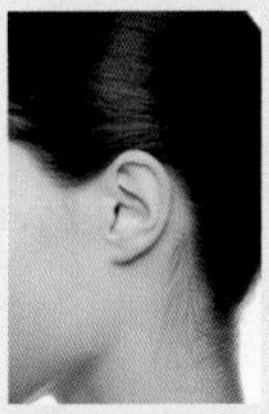

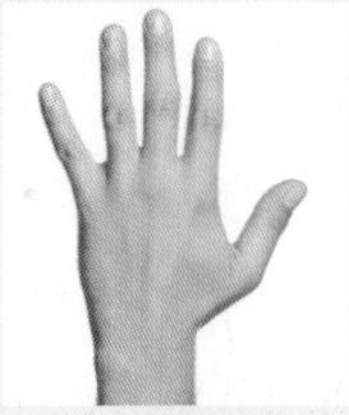

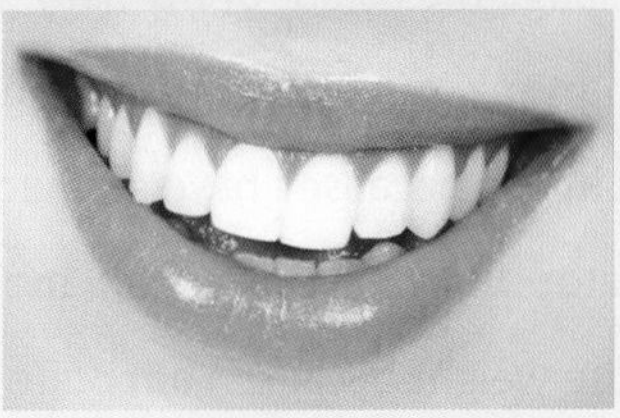

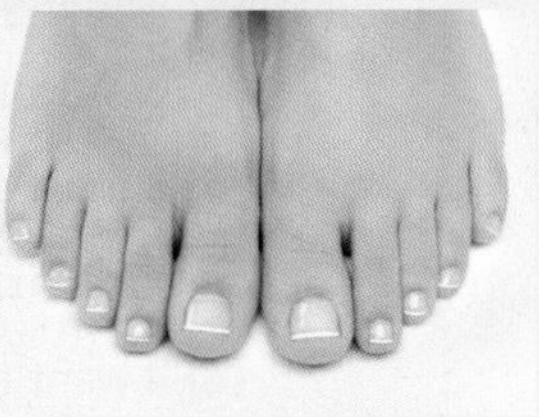

9.5 Write a sentence of between five and ten words for each picture, as in the example.

Example:

- *Je joue au squash pour garder la forme.*

(a)

(b)

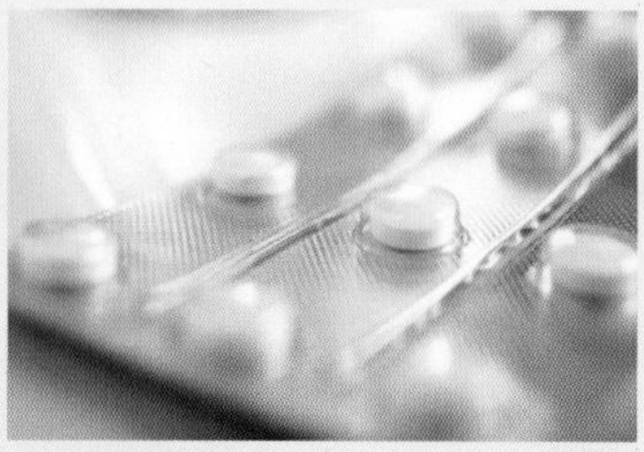

Level 2

9.6 Use the vocabulary provided to help you translate the following sentences into French.

(a) She is telephoning the doctor because Marc is ill.

téléphoner, médecin (m.), malade

(b) My sister is very sporty and she loves to play golf.

sœur (f.), sportif, adorer, jouer, golf (m.)

(c) I want to change the colour of my hair.

vouloir, changer, couleur (f.), cheveu (m.)

(d) I must stay in bed because I have stomach ache.

devoir, rester, lit (m.), ventre (m.), mal (m.)

(e) I want to lose weight because I am quite fat and I am not fit.

vouloir, maigrir, gros, forme (f.)

Level 2

9.7 You are writing to your French friend about your health. Write an email of 80–120 words. You must mention at least four of the following points:

- Une maladie — An illness
- La pharmacie — The chemist's
- Des médicaments — Some medicines
- Un problème — A problem
- Demain — Tomorrow

★ Make sure you know

- ★ Parts of the body
- ★ How to talk about your health
- ★ How to explain health problems to the doctor or chemist

Test yourself 31 ✓

Now you have completed this chapter, make sure you can answer the following questions. Answers are given at the back of the book.

1 Read the following sentences and decide which part of the body each is describing, from the options below.

les mains **la tête** **le genou** **les jambes** **les cheveux**
le nez **la bouche** **les yeux** **les oreilles** **les pieds**

(a) J'en ai besoin pour manger un sandwich.

(b) J'en ai besoin pour courir.

(c) J'en ai besoin pour jouer de la guitare.

(d) J'en ai besoin pour lire un roman.

(e) J'en ai besoin pour me promener.

2 Which of the following would you find in a hospital?

(a) un comprimé

(b) un chien

(c) un maillot de rugby

(d) un infirmier

(e) un autobus

(f) un médecin

(g) du sparadrap

(h) une voiture

(i) une boucherie

(j) une aspirine

Exam-style questions answers

Chapter 3: Family, friends and pets

3.1 The following are examples of possible answers only.

(a) Bonjour Madame Duroc.

(b) Comment allez-vous?

(c) Je vais bien, merci.

(d) Je voudrais/Je vais vous présenter ma famille.

(e) Mon chat s'appelle Peggy.

(f) Avez-vous un chat?

3.2 The following are examples of possible answers only.

(a) Salut Julie.

(b) Ça va bien, merci, et toi?

(c) Rendez-vous où?

(d) Non, je préfère devant la gare.

(e) À demain.

(f) Bonne nuit.

3.3 The following words are examples of possible answers only.

mère, père, frère, grand-mère, grand-père, petits-enfants, bébé, jumeaux, sœur, tante, oncle

3.4 (a) Mes parents habitent dans une petite maison au bord de la mer.

(b) L'enfant rencontre ses cousins derrière le cinéma.

(c) Nous allons chez mes grands-parents la semaine prochaine.

(d) Les dames dans ma famille sont très belles.

(e) Ma mère adore aller au théâtre avec son père.

3.5 The following are examples of possible answers only.

(a) Je m'appelle Gertrude et j'ai treize ans. Je suis assez grande et mince et j'ai les cheveux noirs. Je suis bavarde mais très polie.

(b) Il y a cinq personnes dans ma famille: mon père, ma mère, mes deux frères et moi. Mes frères s'appellent Mark et Peter et je suis la plus petite. J'ai aussi mon petit chien Bob!

(c) J'ai deux frères. Ils s'appellent Mark et Peter et je suis la plus petite.

(d) Mon père est medécin/homme d'affaires/agent de police. Ma mère est secrétaire/femme d'affaires/institutrice.

(Remember: You do not say 'a' in front of a job in French.)

(e) Oui, j'ai un petit chien noir qui s'appelle Bob et cinq cochons d'Inde. Je promène Bob dans la forêt avec ma mère.

Non. Je n'ai pas d'animaux domestiques mais je voudrais une tortue.

(f) Mon meilleur ami (masculine) s'appelle Henry et il a douze ans. Il est très gros, petit et laid. Il a les cheveux roux et courts. Il aime bien jouer aux échecs et il est très bavard.

Ma meilleure amie (feminine) s'appelle Jenny et elle a treize ans. Elle est grande et mince et elle a les cheveux longs, blonds et raides. Elle est très jolie mais elle n'est pas très intelligente.

3.6 (a) Bonjour. Je m'appelle ...

(b) J'habite avec mes parents.

(c) Je suis enfant unique/fils unique/fille unique.

(d) Mon père est grand, mince et très sportif.

(e) Ma mère est dentiste.

(f) Tu as des animaux domestiques?

3.7 In the grid below are all the details about each person. You need to have at least two from each list.

Person	Details
Marc	11 years old; quite long brown hair; blue eyes
Mother	called Françoise; small and thin; red hair; short curly hair
Father	called Philippe; 40 years old; tall and a bit fat; blue eyes; bald
Matthieu	15 years old; very sporty; muscular; tanned; loves playing rugby
Luc	13 years old; very intelligent; brown hair; loves rock music
Jean	5 years old; short blonde hair; quite small; very cute; has freckles

3.8 (a) five

(b) two boys and a girl

(c) long straight (hair)

(d) a teacher

(e) 7.35

3.9
1 H
2 D
3 E
4 A (example)
5 F
6 B

3.10 (a) héros

(b) célèbre

(c) laid

(d) je sens mauvais

(e) chauve

(f) ma nouvelle femme

(g) une ogresse

(h) la plus belle du monde

(i) un gilet

(j) sale

3.11 (a) On a farm in the countryside

(b) Teach him new tricks

(c) A horse

(d) He chases anyone who goes into the field

(e) He was late for school so he took a shortcut

(f) A pear tree

(g) By throwing a pear for Rex to chase

3.12 The following words are examples of possible answers only.

chien, chat, perruche, oiseau, hamster, cochon d'Inde, lapin, cheval, serpent, poisson rouge, perroquet

3.13 (a) Comment t'*appelles*-tu?

(b) Je m'*appelle* Marc.

(c) L'enfant est *grand*.

(d) Mes lunettes sont *brunes*.

(e) J'*habite* à Paris.

3.14 The following are examples of possible answers only.

(a) Voici ma mère avec ma petite sœur qui s'appelle Claire.

(b) Nous avons un grand chien noir et blanc.

Chapter 4: House, home, daily routine and chores

4.1 The following are examples of possible answers only.

(a) Ma maison est grande et jolie.

(b) C'est à la campagne et elle se trouve dans un petit village près de Sherborne.

(c) Il y a cinq chambres, deux salles de bains, un salon, une salle à manger et une cuisine.

(d) Dans ma chambre il y a un petit lit, une armoire, une commode et une assez grande table. Sur la table il y a un ordinateur, des livres et un miroir.

(e) Il y a un jardin derrière/devant/autour de ma maison. Il y a beaucoup de fleurs et des arbres. J'aime bien les pommiers et les sapins.

(f) Ma maison idéale serait très grande avec une piscine en plein air et un jacuzzi. Je voudrais aussi un gymnase et une salle de jeux pour mon frère, ma sœur et moi.

(g) Il y a mon père, ma mère, mes deux frères Philip et Mark, ma sœur Elizabeth et moi.

(h) Oui, j'aime bien ma maison./Non, je ne l'aime pas beaucoup.

(i) Je joue sur l'ordinateur dans ma chambre et je joue au foot dans le jardin avec mon frère/ma sœur. Le week-end, je joue aux échecs avec mon père ou je bavarde avec ma mère.

(j) Le samedi matin je lave la voiture pour mon père et, après ça, je promène le chien dans le bois derrière la maison. Je fais la vaisselle, je mets la table, je range ma chambre et je passe l'aspirateur.

4.2 The following are examples of possible answers only.

(a) J'aime beaucoup ma chambre.

(b) Ma chambre en Angleterre est très petite.

(c) J'habite dans une ferme.

(d) Tu te lèves à quelle heure?

(e) Est-ce que je peux prendre un bain?

(f) Je voudrais me coucher.

4.3 The following are examples of possible answers only.

(a) J'habite dans une maison.

(b) J'habite dans les environs de Londres./J'habite dans la banlieue de Londres.

(c) Il y a quatre chambres dans ma maison.

(d) Il y a un jardin derrière ma maison.

(e) Je lave les voitures.

(f) Quelquefois je fais du babysitting.

4.4 You should have picked the following phrases:

(a) (c) (d) (e) (g) (j)

4.5 (a) TRUE (c) FALSE (e) TRUE
(b) FALSE (d) FALSE (f) FALSE

4.6 You should have picked the following:

(d) (e) (f) (h) (i)

4.7 The following words are examples of possible answers only.

lit, commode, chaise, fenêtre, armoire, télévision, plante, vêtements, bureau, ordinateur, posters, petit ours/ours en peluche, commode

4.8 (a) Ma maison est *grande*.

(b) Le salon est *petit*.

(c) La machine à laver est *blanche*.

(d) Luc *ramasse* ses vêtements.

(e) Maman *prépare* le petit-déjeuner.

4.9 The following are examples of possible answers only.

(a) Nous habitons une grande maison à la campagne.

(b) Je fais mes devoirs tous les soirs avant le dîner.

4.10 (a) Elle fait ses devoirs devant la télévision.

(b) Mon père se brosse les dents dans la salle de bains.

(c) Ma sœur prépare son déjeuner dans la cuisine.

(d) Je tonds la grande pelouse avec mon frère chaque semaine.

(e) Dans ma chambre j'ai six grands posters et trois petites plantes.

4.11 The following is an example of a possible answer only.

Cher Jean-Paul,

Comment vas-tu? J'espère que tu vas venir bientôt chez moi.

J'habite une assez grande maison près du centre-ville. J'aime beaucoup habiter ici parce qu'il y a beaucoup de magasins tout près et je peux promener le chien dans le parc en face.

Nous avons une très grande cuisine et un salon au rez-de-chaussée et au premier étage il y a quatre chambres. Ma chambre est petite mais je l'aime bien. Derrière la maison il y a un jardin où j'aime lire quand il fait beau.

Hier, l'école a fini à quatre heures et je suis rentré tout de suite. J'ai pris mon goûter et puis j'ai promené le chien. Le soir, j'ai fait mes devoirs avant le dîner puis j'ai lu et j'ai regardé la télé. Je me suis couché à neuf heures et demie.

Demain matin, je vais me lever à sept heures et quart. Je vais prendre mon petit-déjeuner vers huit heures moins le quart – un jus de fruit et des céréales – et je vais quitter la maison à huit heures vingt. Je vais aller à l'école à pied car elle n'est pas loin de chez moi.

À bientôt, John

Chapter 5: In town, travel and transport, food and drink

5.1 The following are examples of possible answers only.

(a) Il y a beaucoup de choses à faire près de chez moi. Ma sœur aime faire les magasins en ville mais, moi, j'adore faire du bowling et puis aller au cinéma.

(b) Non, je n'aime pas faire du shopping. Je préfère aller à la patinoire./Oui, je vais en ville chaque week-end avec mes ami(e)s et j'achète de nouveaux vêtements.

(c) J'achète mes bonbons à la petite confiserie sur la place principale en ville.

5.2 (a) Je voudrais changer de l'argent.
(b) J'ai des livres sterling.
(c) Je voudrais deux cents euros.
(d) Oui, j'ai mon passeport.
(e) Est-ce que la banque est ouverte le samedi?
(f) À quelle heure ouvre la banque le lundi?

5.3 (a) Où se trouve le supermarché?
(b) Est-ce qu'il s'appelle Carrefour?
(c) C'est loin d'ici?
(d) C'est le grand bâtiment à droite?
(e) Est-ce qu'il y a une poste près d'ici?
(f) Est-ce qu'il y a une boîte aux lettres près d'ici?

5.4 (a) post office
(b) tourist office
(c) delicatessen
(d) chemist's
(e) church

5.5 (a) TRUE
(b) FALSE
(c) TRUE
(d) FALSE
(e) FALSE

5.6

(a) *La pharmacie*	**La banque**	(b) *La librairie*	**L'épicerie**	(c) *La poissonnerie*
		La rue		
(d) *Le supermarché*	**La poste**	(e) *La boulangerie*	(f) *Le cinéma*	(g) *La pâtisserie*

5.7 (a) Amélie
(b) Pierre
(c) Jean
(d) Philippe
(e) Anne

5.8 The following words are examples of possible answers only.

école, église, poste, restaurant, librairie, boucherie, boulangerie, supermarché, parking, piscine, banque

5.9 (a) La pharmacie se trouve en face de la vieille église en ville.
(b) Je voudrais un paquet de bonbons jaunes, s'il vous plaît.
(c) Prenez la première rue à gauche après le cinéma.
(d) L'école est fermée pendant les vacances.
(e) Il y a un grand parking devant la piscine.

5.10 The following are examples of possible answers only.
(a) Je préfère voyager en voiture car c'est confortable.
(b) Je préfère voyager en avion car c'est plus rapide.
(c) À mon avis, le moyen de transport le plus confortable est l'avion.

5.11 (a) Je voudrais un billet deuxième classe pour Paris, s'il vous plaît.

(b) Non, un aller-retour.

(c) À quelle heure est-ce que le prochain train part?

(d) De quel quai part le train?

(e) À quelle heure est-ce que le train arrive à Paris?

(f) Est-ce que je dois changer?

5.12 (a) Je voudrais aller à Lille demain.

(b) Est-ce qu'il y a un train vers midi?

(c) Est-ce qu'il arrive à Lille avant quatorze heures?

(d) C'est très rapide.

(e) Est-ce que c'est direct?

(f) Je voudrais un aller simple, s'il vous plaît.

5.13 (a) Je voyage en bus.

(b) Le bus est en retard.

(c) Le bus va arriver à onze heures.

(d) On va/Je vais arriver devant l'église.

(e) Le billet coûte dix euros.

(f) À bientôt.

5.14 (a) Je dois acheter quatre billets pour ma famille.

(b) Le prochain train part à quelle heure?

(c) Maman stationne notre voiture rouge devant la grande statue.

(d) On peut acheter des fleurs jaunes au supermarché.

(e) Henri aime lire des livres à la bibliothèque.

5.15 The following is an example of a possible answer only.

Chère Anne,

Nous sommes bien arrivés à Versailles.

Nous avons pris le train de Reading à Londres, puis le métro à la Gare de St Pancras. Notre Eurostar est parti à dix-sept heures et nous sommes arrivés deux heures plus tard à Paris. Le voyage sous la Manche est très rapide. Je dois dire que le train est le moyen de transport que je préfère. Le train est confortable, il y a un buffet, et il n'y a pas de retard quand il fait du brouillard.

Quand nous sommes descendus du train à la Gare du Nord, nous avons attendu nos amis qui devaient venir nous chercher, mais ils ne sont pas venus. Où étaient-ils? Finalement ils nous ont téléphoné pour nous dire que leur voiture était en panne. Nous avons dû prendre un taxi à Versailles et cela nous a coûté cher! Papa n'était pas content.

J'adore rester chez nos amis à Versailles. La maman est anglaise et son mari est français. Ils ont une fille qui a le même âge que moi et un petit chien adorable.

À Versailles il y a beaucoup de choses à voir. La ville est très jolie et il y a le château magnifique avec ses beaux jardins. Nous allons visiter le château demain matin. Ça va être formidable!

Bisous, Marie

5.16 The following are examples of possible answers only.

(a) Je prends le petit-déjeuner à sept heures trente.

(b) J'adore les bananes.

(c) Je préfère le jambon mais j'aime aussi l'agneau.

(d) J'aime les sandwichs au fromage.

(e) Normalement je bois de l'eau minérale mais, quelquefois, je bois du jus d'orange.

5.17 (a) Je voudrais une table près de la fenêtre, s'il vous plaît.

(b) Une limonade et un jus de pomme, s'il vous plaît.

(c) Je voudrais du melon, s'il vous plaît.

(d) Je prends le poulet-frites.

(e) Qu'est-ce que vous avez comme dessert?

(f) Deux glaces à la vanille, s'il vous plaît.

5.18 (a) Je voudrais une table pour cinq personnes, s'il vous plaît.

(b) Pas près de la porte.

(c) La table est sale.

(d) Mes parents voudraient une bouteille de vin rouge.

(e) Je voudrais un verre de limonade.

(f) Je n'ai pas de serviette (de table).

5.19 (a) 5

(b) 2

(c) 4

(d) 6

(e) 3

5.20

	Le Bosquet	Chez Pierre	Le Petit Lapin
Chips			✓
Duck	✓		
Rice		✓	
Egg			✓
Goat's cheese	✓		
Apple	✓		

5.21 The following words are examples of possible answers only.

sandwich, pomme, banane, gâteau, chips, bonbons, frites, fromage, poisson, œufs, glace

5.22 (a) Je voudrais une *petite* bouteille de limonade, s'il vous plaît.

(b) Tu voudrais un chocolat *chaud*?

(c) Il *voudrait* un sandwich au fromage.

(d) Elle *mange* une grande tranche de pizza.

(e) Je *prends* une tarte aux pommes, s'il vous plaît.

5.23 The following are examples of possible answers only.

(a) Je vais au marché tous les samedis avec Maman.

(b) L'été dernier nous avons voyagé à Paris en train.

(c) J'aime voyager en avion parce que c'est très rapide.

5.24 (a) J'adore le saumon mais ne n'aime pas la truite.

(b) Je voudrais un sandwich au jambon pour ma sœur.

(c) Maman achète une douzaine de croissants en ville.

(d) Papa préfère le thé au lait mais je déteste les boissons chaudes.

(e) Les bananes sont jaunes mais les fraises sont rouges.

5.25 The following is an example of a possible answer only.

Chère Madeleine,

Nous avons passé une journée formidable à Édimbourg le week-end dernier pour fêter mon anniversaire. Nous habitons à la campagne alors c'est toujours un plaisir de visiter la ville.

Je me suis levée de bonne heure et j'ai pris mon petit-déjeuner en vitesse: un chocolat chaud, des toasts et de la confiture d'oranges. Est-ce que tu aimes la confiture d'oranges?

À huit heures et demie nous sommes partis en voiture à Édimbourg. Il faisait beau et le paysage était très joli. Les petits agneaux dans les champs avaient l'air content! Nous sommes arrivés une heure plus tard et nous avons trouvé un parking au centre-ville.

Il y avait beaucoup de monde, surtout dans la vieille ville. J'ai vu des touristes américains, japonais, allemands, et même français! J'ai voulu visiter le château mais nous ne sommes pas entrés parce que Papa a dit que c'était un peu cher. Alors nous sommes allés au musée des jouets – c'était très amusant!

À midi nous avons déjeuné dans un petit restaurant où j'ai pris un steak-frites délicieux. Comme dessert il y avait un grand choix de glaces. On a vraiment bien mangé!

L'année prochaine, je vais retourner à Édimbourg avec ma meilleure amie. On va voyager en train parce que c'est pratique et assez rapide. Le matin, on va faire du shopping et l'après-midi on va visiter le château. Ça va être une journée fatigante mais superbe!

Écris-moi bientôt,

Amitiés,

Laura

Chapter 6: Free time

6.1 The following are examples of possible answers only.

(a) Je joue au rugby/foot/golf/netball/tennis.

Je fais de la natation./Je nage.

Je fais de l'équitation./Je fais du cheval.

Je collectionne des timbres.

Je fais du vélo/VTT.

Je fais de la voile/planche à voile.

(b) Je joue au rugby/foot/golf/netball/tennis.

Je fais de la natation./Je nage.

Je fais de l'équitation./Je fais du cheval.

(c) Je préfère jouer au squash.

(d) Je préfère la musique pop/la musique classique/le jazz/le hard. C'est cool et j'aime bien Britney/Mozart, etc.

(e) Oui, je joue de la trompette depuis deux ans.

(f) Je vais au cinéma avec mes copains deux fois par mois.

(g) Quand je suis avec mes copains je vais au parc et je fais du skate.

(h) Le week-end prochain je vais aller chez mon oncle et ma tante car c'est l'anniversaire de mon cousin Max.

(i) J'aime jouer au foot dans le jardin.

J'adore lire mes livres dans ma chambre.

(j) Je me suis levé à dix heures.

J'ai joué au foot dans le jardin avec mon ami Fred.

(k) Je fais du shopping en ville avec ma copine Marie.

Je mange beaucoup de fast-food devant la télé.

6.2 The following are examples of possible answers only.

(a) Tu veux aller au cinéma?

(b) Il y a un film d'aventures à quinze heures.

(c) C'est un film avec Tom Cruise.

(d) Rendez-vous devant le cinéma.

(e) Rendez-vous à quatorze heures trente.

(f) Tu veux aller en ville après?

6.3 (a) Wednesday evening

(b) She has to go to her grandmother's house as it is her grandmother's birthday; Anne does not like science fiction films

(c) A rugby match

(d) Opposite the library

(e) There are fewer people

(f) About 1.30 p.m

6.4 (a) From time to time

(b) A film called *Maman, j'ai raté l'avion* (*Home Alone*)

(c) There are too many people/He prefers staying at home with his family and dogs/He does not like popcorn

(d) Action films

(e) Gérard Depardieu

(f) He fell asleep

(g) A magician

(h) Ugly

(i) He is very romantic

6.5 (a) 3

(b) 5

(c) 4

(d) 8

(e) 2

(f) 6

6.6 (a) 4

(b) 7

(c) 9

(d) 8

(e) 3

(f) 1

(g) 2

(h) 6

(i) 5

6.7 (a) 2

(b) 4

(c) 3

(d) 5

(e) 1

6.8 The following words are examples of possible answers only.

piano, netball, télévision, cartes, échecs, foot, batterie, ping-pong, basket, ordinateur, livres

6.9 (a) J'*aime* jouer au netball.

(b) Elle *dessine* dans sa chambre.

(c) Est-ce que tu *fais* de l'athlétisme?

(d) Son ballon est *bleu*.

(e) Papa lit une histoire *amusante*.

6.10 The following are examples of possible answers only.

(a) Hier j'ai joué au squash avec mon ami Henri.

(b) Je joue de la trompette depuis trois ans.

(c) Le week-end dernier ma famille et moi sommes allés au théâtre.

6.11 The following are examples of possible answers only.

Je suis très sportif/sportive et j'aime beaucoup le sport.

J'adore aller à la piscine avec mes amis car j'aime nager.

Je fais de la voile le samedi matin avec Papa.

Je préfère jouer au foot mais j'aime aussi faire du ski.

Je n'aime pas regarder la télévision mais j'aime lire des romans.

6.12 (a) Je joue du piano mais mes deux sœurs jouent de la batterie.

(b) Mon frère aime lire des magazines mais je préfère les autobiographies.

(c) Ma chanteuse préférée est française.

(d) Mon oncle est acteur et il aime les westerns.

(e) Ma tante chante et elle adore la musique classique.

6.13 The following is an example of a possible answer only.

Cher Philippe,

Demain, c'est l'anniversaire de mon ami Stephen. Je suis allé en ville le week-end dernier pour lui acheter un cadeau. Malheureusement, j'ai oublié mon porte-monnaie et j'ai dû retourner à la maison! En tout cas, je n'avais pas beaucoup d'argent, alors mon père m'a donné quelques euros. J'ai visité de nombreux magasins, mais je n'ai pas trouvé un bon cadeau pour mon ami. J'étais très vexé! Mais quand je passais devant le stade j'ai eu une bonne idée. Je suis allé au guichet et j'ai acheté deux billets pour le match de demain après-midi.

Stephen va être très content de ce cadeau parce qu'il adore le football et notre équipe préférée va jouer dans le match. À mon avis, notre équipe va gagner! On va très bien s'amuser!

Amitiés,

Paul

Chapter 7: Life and work at school

7.1 The following are examples of possible answers only.

(a) J'arrive à l'école à huit heures et quart et nous avons l'appel à huit heures et demie. Le premier cours commence à neuf heures et il y a trois cours avant la récré qui est à onze heures. Je prends mon déjeuner à la cantine à une heure moins dix et, après ça, il y a une autre récré. Je fais du sport pendant l'après-midi. En été je joue au cricket et je fais de l'athlétisme. Je rentre à la maison à cinq heures, je prends mon goûter puis je fais mes devoirs.

(b) Nous avons huit cours par jour.

(c) Les devoirs durent une heure.

(d) J'aime l'histoire et la géo parce qu'elles sont intéressantes et je les trouve faciles mais je préfère les maths car le prof est très gentil et je suis fort(e) en maths.

(e) Mon école est assez grande et elle se trouve à Londres. C'est une école mixte avec deux cents élèves. À l'école il y a beaucoup de salles de classe, un gymnase, une cantine, une bibliothèque, des terrains de sport et des courts de tennis. Malheureusement, il n'y a pas de piscine.

(f) J'aime bien mon école car les profs sont gentils et il y a beaucoup de choses à faire./Je n'aime pas mon école car les cours sont ennuyeux.

(g) Pendant la récréation je joue au foot/je bavarde avec mes amis/je lis/je joue au tennis.

(h) J'aime jouer au foot./J'aime bavarder avec mes amis./J'aime lire./J'aime jouer au tennis.

(i) Cet après-midi je vais jouer au cricket.

(j) Hier c'était dimanche donc je suis resté(e) chez moi avec ma famille.

(k) Comme uniforme je porte un pantalon noir, une chemise bleue, un pull gris et une cravate bleue.

7.2 (a) Je n'ai pas de stylo.

(b) Tu as une règle?

(c) Quelle est la date?

(d) Le professeur parle trop vite.

(e) À quelle heure finit le cours?

(f) Les cours sont très longs en France.

7.3 (a) L'école est très grande.

(b) Il y a combien d'élèves?

(c) Mon école est plus petite.

(d) Il y a quatre-vingts garçons et cinquante-cinq filles.

(e) À quelle heure commence le premier cours?

(f) Les cours commencent à huit heures et demie à mon école.

7.4 (a) Je peux entrer?

(b) Je loge chez mon correspondant/ma correspondante.

(c) J'ai treize ans.

(d) Je suis ici pour une semaine.

(e) Est-ce que je dois faire les devoirs?

(f) On fait les devoirs tous les jours en Angleterre.

7.5 (a) 3
(b) 2
(c) 3
(d) 2
(e) 1

7.6 (a) boys and girls
(b) 170
(c) physics
(d) short curly hair
(e) drama

7.7 (a) 4
(b) 3
(c) 5
(d) 2
(e) 6

7.8

	TRUE	FALSE
Example: Jean-Paul is 13 years old.	✓	
(a) His school is in the south-east of England.		✓
(b) There are 180 pupils in his school.		✓
(c) He does not like Latin.		✓
(d) He does homework five times a week.	✓	
(e) He really likes swimming.	✓	

7.9 Mon école s'appelle Brockett Hall. C'est une école privée et *mixte*. Il y a environ deux cents *élèves* de huit à *treize* ans et douze professeurs. Mon école est bien équipée. Par exemple, il y a un nouveau gymnase et la *bibliothèque* a été construite il y a dix-huit mois. Je ne suis pas très *sportif* mais j'adore la lecture.

J'arrive à l'école à huit *heures* vingt et les cours *commencent* quinze minutes plus tard. Il y a une récré à onze heures moins cinq et ça *dure* vingt-cinq minutes. Il y a beaucoup de *clubs* pendant la pause-déjeuner. Pour les élèves qui aiment les sports, il y a des clubs comme le rugby et le netball mais, moi, j'aime jouer aux *échecs*.

Ma matière préférée, c'est l'histoire et je m'intéresse beaucoup à la Deuxième Guerre mondiale. J'ai horreur des sciences parce que le professeur n'est pas *patient*. Je trouve les *expériences* fatigantes et nous avons fait un *test* hier matin.

7.10 The following words are examples of possible answers only.

crayons, stylo, livre, règle, calculatrice, chaise, bureau, sac, ordinateur, gomme, trousse

7.11 (a) Je *veux* jouer sur l'ordinateur.

(b) Anne-Marie *bavarde* avec ses amies dans la salle de classe.

(c) Il *déteste* l'histoire car le prof est très strict.

(d) *Ferme* la fenêtre, s'il te plaît, Henri.

(e) Les chaises dans ma salle de classe sont *bleues*.

7.12 The following are examples of possible answers only.

(a) Ma matière préférée est l'histoire parce que le professeur est drôle.

(b) J'adore la musique mais je ne chante pas bien.

7.13 The following are examples of possible answers only.

Ma matière préférée, c'est la biologie car c'est intéressant.

Je n'aime pas les maths parce que le professeur est très strict et il crie beaucoup.

J'ai beaucoup de devoirs ce soir et je suis fatigué(e).

J'aime le latin car j'adore les histoires mais je n'aime pas beaucoup la grammaire.

Je suis assez faible en physique, chimie et biologie mais mon amie Ellen adore les sciences.

7.14 (a) Les cours commencent à neuf heures.

(b) Je préfère les maths parce que le professeur est amusant.

(c) Mes amis sont internes mais je suis externe.

(d) Le directeur est très strict mais il est aussi assez sportif.

(e) J'adore jouer au netball et ma mère aime regarder les matchs.

7.15 The following is an example of a possible answer only.

Chère Anne,

Merci beaucoup pour ta lettre. Je vais te parler de mon école.

Mon école se trouve dans la banlieue. J'habite assez près de l'école alors j'y vais à pied normalement.

Ma matière préférée est le français parce que c'est intéressant et je suis assez forte en langues. J'adore aussi le dessin parce que c'est très amusant, mais je n'aime pas les maths car à mon avis c'est difficile.

Deux fois par semaine, nous faisons du sport. J'adore ça, surtout en été quand nous jouons au tennis. En hiver, nous jouons au hockey. Il y a beaucoup de clubs à l'école. Moi, je vais au club de musique chaque jeudi pendant la pause-déjeuner. Je joue de la guitare depuis deux ans.

Hier, les cours ont commencé à huit heures et demie. Le matin, avant la récré, j'ai eu deux cours de sciences et un cours de latin. Après la récré, j'ai eu histoire et anglais. C'était fatigant.

Demain, après l'école, mes amies et moi vont faire de la natation. Tu aimes la natation? Nous avons une piscine magnifique à l'école, alors n'oublie pas ton maillot de bain! Puis je vais rentrer tout de suite chez moi parce que j'ai beaucoup de devoirs.

Et toi, comment est ton école? Écris-moi bientôt.

Amicalement,

Sophie

Chapter 8: Holidays, weather, time and dates

8.1 The following are examples of possible answers only.

(a) Quel temps fait-il là-bas?

(b) Ici il fait chaud, mais il pleut.

(c) Quelle est la date de ton anniversaire?

(d) Qu'est que tu vas faire à Noël?

(e) J'adore faire du ski en hiver.

(f) Au revoir.

8.2 You should have picked the following:

(a) (i)

8.3 (a) 2

(b) 2

(c) 2

(d) 3

(e) 1

8.4 (a) Il est neuf heures cinq.

(b) Il est neuf heures et demie.

(c) Il est neuf heures vingt.

(d) Il est neuf heures moins le quart.

(e) Il est neuf heures et quart.

8.5 The following words are examples of possible answers only.

soleil, neige, pluie, vent, nuage/nuageux, froid, arc-en-ciel, éclair/orage, brouillard, glace

8.6 (a) Il *fait* beau aujourd'hui.

(b) Il *est* trois heures trente.

(c) Tu *es* en retard.

(d) Marc va partir la semaine *prochaine*.

(e) Le ciel est *couvert*.

8.7 The following are examples of possible answers only.

Ma fête préférée, c'est Noël.

Je fête Noël à la maison avec ma famille.

On a des cadeaux et on mange un gros repas.

J'aime aussi Pâques parce que j'adore le chocolat!

L'année prochaine je voudrais aller à une fête de musique.

8.8 The following are examples of possible answers only.

(a) Pendant les grandes vacances j'aime aller à la plage avec mes copains. J'aime aller chez mon oncle Harry qui habite à Londres.

(b) Je me lève à dix heures et je me douche. Je prends mon petit-déjeuner devant la télé et puis je joue sur l'ordinateur jusqu'à midi. Après mon déjeuner je vais en ville ou à la plage avec mes copains et je m'amuse bien.

(c) Je vais à la plage avec mes copains ou je joue au foot dans le parc.

(d) Je suis allé(e) en France/Écosse/Allemagne.

Je suis allé(e) au Japon/Canada.

Je suis allé(e) aux États-Unis.

(e) Je suis allé(e) en France avec ma famille et nous avons loué un gîte dans le sud. Nous sommes allé(e)s à la plage chaque jour et nous avons nagé.

8.9 (a) Bonjour. Je m'appelle John.
(b) Il fait très chaud aujourd'hui.
(c) Où habites-tu?
(d) Est-ce qu'il fait toujours beau?
(e) Oui, je suis ici pour deux semaines.
(f) Je passe mes vacances ici chaque année.

8.10 (a) Je voudrais un emplacement, s'il vous plaît.
(b) Nous avons une tente.
(c) Il y a cinq personnes dans ma famille.
(d) Nous voulons rester quatre nuits.
(e) Où se trouve le bloc sanitaire?
(f) Est-ce qu'il y a une piscine?

8.11 (a) Vous avez des chambres libres?
(b) C'est pour deux adultes et trois enfants.
(c) C'est combien?
(d) Est-ce qu'il y a une douche dans la chambre?
(e) Est-ce qu'on peut manger à l'hôtel maintenant?
(f) Est-ce qu'il y a un restaurant près d'ici?

8.12 (a) 4 (c) 3
(b) 1 (d) 2

8.13 (a) A week
(b) There was an accident with the tent because it was too windy
(c) Five
(d) Ice creams for everyone
(e) He was tired so he lay down on it for 15 minutes
(f) Prepare a barbecue
(g) The pitch was next to a wood so barbecues were forbidden

8.14 (a) It was built in 1889
(b) For the Universal Exhibition (World Fair) in Paris/to celebrate 100 years since the French Revolution
(c) It is 300 metres tall
(d) To protest against it being built
(e) Because it has antennae for French radio and television

8.15 The following are examples of possible answers only.
(a) Pendant les vacances de Noël j'ai fait du ski.
(b) Nous allons faire du camping au bord de la mer.

8.16 (a) Le soleil brille et je regarde la télévision.
(b) C'est l'anniversaire de ma mère et mon père fait un gâteau.
(c) Il est neuf heures et je vais acheter un journal.

(d) Je suis dans un grand hôtel et il y a une belle vue sur la mer.

(e) Il y a quatre douches et trente tentes au camping.

8.17 The following is an example of a possible answer only.

Salut Marc,

Nous nous amusons ici dans notre gîte. Je vais te raconter notre journée à la plage hier.

Après le petit-déjeuner nous avons pris le bus pour aller à une petite plage à trois kilomètres du gîte et nous avons passé toute la matinée dans la mer. À midi nous sommes allés au restaurant en ville, à côté de la plage, où nous avons mangé des fruits de mer délicieux et des glaces au chocolat. L'après-midi nous avons joué avec le grand ballon rouge que Papa a acheté dans un petit kiosque. Il y avait beaucoup de touristes sur la plage et malheureusement, quand mon frère a lancé le ballon, il est tombé sur une vieille dame qui dormait au soleil. Elle était très fâchée! Mes parents aussi. Le soir, quand nous sommes rentrés au gîte nous avons dû lire des magazines parce que Papa avait confisqué le ballon!

Demain matin, s'il fait beau, nous allons faire une randonnée et un pique-nique à la campagne. S'il fait mauvais, nous allons acheter des souvenirs et des cartes postales en ville.

Écris-moi bientôt,

Charles

8.18 The following are examples of possible answers only.

Lundi:	Je suis arrivé(e) à l'hôtel et je suis très fatigué(e).
Mardi:	Aujourd'hui nous avons fait du shopping et j'ai acheté un nouveau T-shirt.
Mercredi:	Nous sommes allé(e)s à l'aquarium ce matin car il pleuvait.
Jeudi:	Le soleil brillait donc Papa a loué un petit bateau.
Vendredi:	Encore du soleil alors ma sœur a bronzé sur le balcon.
Samedi:	J'ai joué au foot dans le parc avec des touristes italiens.
Dimanche:	Nous avons fait nos valises parce que nous allons partir demain matin.

Chapter 9: Health and fitness

9.1 The following are examples of possible answers only.

(a) Je suis malade.

(b) J'ai mal à la tête.

(c) J'ai très chaud.

(d) Oui. Est-ce que je peux téléphoner au médecin?

(e) Je reste chez mon ami(e) français(e).

(f) Comment s'appelle le médecin?

9.2 (a) J'ai mal à l'oreille.

(b) Je ne peux pas dormir.

(c) Je n'ai pas faim.

(d) Où se trouve la pharmacie?

(e) Est-ce que la pharmacie est ouverte aujourd'hui?

(f) Puis-je avoir du paracétamol?

9.3 (a) Cathérine

(b) Marc

(c) Anne

(d) Martine

(e) Paul

9.4 The following words are examples of possible answers only.

ventre, bras, tête, nez, yeux, oreille, main, dents, genou, pied, jambe

9.5 The following are examples of possible answers only.

(a) Je vais me coucher parce que j'ai mal à la tête.

(b) Quand maman a mal à la tête elle prend de l'aspirine.

9.6 (a) Elle téléphone au médecin parce que Marc est malade.

(b) Ma sœur est très sportive et elle adore jouer au golf.

(c) Je veux changer la couleur de mes cheveux.

(d) Je dois rester au lit parce que j'ai mal au ventre.

(e) Je veux maigrir parce que je suis assez gros(se) et je ne suis pas en forme.

9.7 The following is an example of a possible answer only.

Salut Lucie,

Ça va?

Malheureusement, moi, ça ne va pas. Je suis enrhumée depuis hier – j'ai mal à la gorge, j'ai mal à la tête, j'ai très chaud et je ne veux pas manger. Ce matin, mon père est allé à la pharmacie et il a acheté des médicaments pour moi, par exemple des paracétamols, des pastilles et du sirop pour la gorge.

Mais il y a un problème parce que le week-end prochain, c'est l'anniversaire de ma meilleure amie. Nous voulons aller au cinéma et manger au fast-food. J'espère que je vais être en forme!

Demain, je ne vais pas aller à l'école car je suis trop malade. (C'est bien parce que j'ai sciences le matin et je n'ai pas fait mes devoirs!) Je vais rester au lit et ma mère va téléphoner au médecin.

Écris-moi bientôt!

Bisous,

Emma

Test yourself answers

Chapter 1: Grammar section

Test yourself 1

(a) J'*aime* jouer au squash.

I like playing squash.

(b) Tu *regardes* le film ce soir?

Are you watching the film this evening?

(c) Il *travaille* dans le jardin.

He is working in the garden.

(d) Elle *mange* un sandwich au jambon.

She is eating a ham sandwich.

(e) Nous *préférons* la robe rose.

We prefer the pink dress.

(f) Vous *écoutez* la radio?

Are you listening/Do you listen to the radio?

(g) Ils *entrent* dans la salle de classe.

They are going into the classroom.

(h) Elles *habitent* dans un appartement.

They live in a flat.

Test yourself 2

(a) Je *choisis* une glace.

I am choosing an ice cream.

(b) Tu *finis* tes devoirs?

Are you finishing your homework?

(c) Il *punit* les élèves méchants.

He is punishing the naughty pupils.

(d) Elle *réussit* tout le temps.

She always succeeds.

(e) Nous *grossissons*.

We are putting on weight.

(f) Vous *maigrissez*?

Are you losing weight?

(g) Ils *finissent* les exercices dans la salle de classe.

The are finishing the exercises in the classroom.

(h) Elles *choisissent* de nouveaux vêtements.

They are choosing some new clothes.

Test yourself 3

(a) Je *tonds* la pelouse.
I am mowing the lawn.

(b) Tu *entends* les enfants?
Can you hear the children?

(c) Il *descend* l'escalier.
He is going downstairs/down the stairs.

(d) Elle *répond* aux questions.
She is replying to the questions.

(e) Nous *attendons* une réponse à notre message électronique.
We are waiting for a reply to our email.

(f) Vous *vendez* des glaces?
Do you sell ice creams?

(g) Ils *vendent* des légumes au marché.
They sell vegetables at the market.

(h) Elles *descendent* de l'autobus devant l'église.
They are getting off the bus in front of the church.

Test yourself 4

(a) Je *m'habille* dans ma chambre.
I get dressed in my bedroom.

(b) Tu *te lèves* à sept heures trente.
You get up at half past seven.

(c) Il *se rase* devant un miroir.
He shaves in front of a mirror.

(d) Elle *se brosse* les dents dans la salle de bains.
She brushes her teeth in the bathroom.

(e) Nous *nous réveillons* très tôt chaque matin.
We wake up very early every morning.

(f) Vous *vous réveillez* à quelle heure?
At what time do you wake up?

(g) Ils *se coiffent* après le petit-déjeuner.
They do their hair after breakfast.

(h) Elles *s'intéressent* à l'histoire.
They are interested in history.

Test yourself 5

(a) Elle *est* grande.
She is tall.

(b) Nous *avons* une petite maison.
We have a small house.

(c) Il *fait* du ski.
He goes skiing.

(d) Nous *allons* au supermarché.
We go to the supermarket.

(e) Ils *sont* amusants.

They are amusing/funny.

(f) Elles *ont* les cheveux longs.

They have long hair.

(g) Tu *vas* au théâtre.

You go to the theatre.

(h) Vous *faites* du vélo.

You go cycling.

(i) Je *suis* très contente.

I am very happy.

(j) J'*ai* deux frères.

I have two brothers.

Test yourself 6

(a) Elle a tort.

(b) Pierre a peur des vaches.

(c) Tu as très chaud.

(d) Ma mère a raison.

(e) J'ai besoin d'un stylo.

Test yourself 7

(a) Je *suis* très contente.

I am very glad/content/pleased.

(b) Tu *as* quel âge?

How old are you?

(c) Il *met* une chemise bleue.

He is putting on a blue shirt.

(d) Elle *ouvre* la porte.

She is opening the door.

(e) Nous *écrivons* une lettre à notre oncle.

We are writing a letter to our uncle.

(f) Vous *voulez* quelque chose à boire?

Do you want something to drink?

(g) Ils *vont* au cinéma ce soir.

They are going to the cinema this evening.

(h) Elles *viennent* chez nous à dix-neuf heures.

They are coming to our house at 7 p.m.

Test yourself 8

(a) Je veux sortir.

(b) Tu aimes jouer au tennis?

(c) Nous pouvons aller au cinéma.

(d) Je voudrais habiter en France.

(e) Je déteste faire les courses.

(f) Elle doit rester à la maison.

Test yourself 9
(a) Elle va arriver cet après-midi.
(b) Ils vont jouer sur l'ordinateur.
(c) Il va s'habiller.
(d) Nous allons choisir un livre.
(e) Est-ce que tu vas retourner en France l'année prochaine?
(f) Vous allez chanter ce soir.
(g) Paul va danser avec Anne.
(h) Elles vont jouer aux cartes après le déjeuner.

Test yourself 10
(a) Je viens de manger.
(b) Elle vient de finir.
(c) Nous sommes en train de boire.
(d) Elles sont en train de choisir.
(e) Matthieu est sur le point d'écrire une lettre.
(f) Il est sur le point de commencer le match.
(g) Je voudrais aller au cinéma.
(h) Tu devrais manger un sandwich.

Test yourself 11
(a) *J'ai fini* mes devoirs. I finished my homework.
(b) *J'ai attendu* l'autobus. I waited for the bus.
(c) *Il a joué* aux cartes. He played cards.
(d) *Elle a choisi* de nouvelles chaussures. She chose some new shoes.
(e) *Nous avons regardé* la télé. We watched television.
(f) *Vous avez entendu* le bruit. You heard the noise.
(g) *Ils ont répondu* aux questions. They replied to the questions.
(h) *Elles ont écouté* de la musique. They listened to some music.

Test yourself 12
(a) J'ai bu de la limonade.
(b) Elle a conduit la voiture.
(c) Il a fait ses devoirs.
(d) Tu as écrit une lettre.
(e) Vous avez lu un magazine.
(f) Nous avons couru très vite.
(g) Ils ont mis les vêtements dans leur chambre.
(h) Elles ont eu un accident.

Test yourself 13
(a) Je suis parti(e) à trois heures.
(b) Elle est sortie à six heures quinze/et quart.
(c) Il est arrivé à l'hôpital avec ses parents.
(d) Nous sommes descendu(e)s à la cuisine.
(e) Vous êtes allé(e)s au cinéma hier soir?
(f) Ils sont venus au café avec leurs amis.
(g) Elles sont entrées dans le salon.
(h) Tu es rentré(e) à quatre heures moins dix.

Test yourself 14
(a) Nous avons fini.
(b) Elle est partie.
(c) Nous sommes venu(e)s.
(d) Elle a joué.
(e) Les garçons sont tombés.

Test yourself 15
(a) Elle s'est habillée dans sa chambre.
(b) Pierre s'est cassé la jambe.
(c) Il s'est lavé dans la salle de bains.
(d) Nous nous sommes couché(e)s après le film.
(e) Elles se sont disputées.
(f) Ils se sont promenés dans le parc.
(g) Tu t'es levé(e) très tôt.
(h) Vous vous êtes sauvé(e)s l'année dernière.
(i) Nous nous sommes assises sous un arbre.

Test yourself 16
(a) Il écoutait de la musique.
(b) Nous regardions la télé.
(c) Elles travaillaient dans une ferme.
(d) Ils jouaient au cricket.
(e) Tu lisais une lettre dans le bureau.
(f) Vous écoutiez la radio?
(g) Il faisait froid.
(h) Elle était professeur.

Test yourself 17
(a) I have not eaten anything.
(b) She is not happy/pleased.
(c) We did not see the lions.
(d) He never drinks lemonade.
(e) We do not have any more bananas.

Test yourself 18
(a) We did not see anyone.
(b) Nobody understands the passage.
(c) I saw neither Pierre nor Louise.
(d) It is only on Saturday evenings that we go to the cinema.
(e) He only goes to his favourite café.

Test yourself 19
(a) un
(b) la
(c) des
(d) de l'
(e) du
(f) une
(g) des
(h) aux
(i) à la
(j) à l'
(k) du
(l) aux

Test yourself 20
(a) rouge
(b) délicieuse
(c) bonne
(d) gentille
(e) petite … brune
(f) intelligents
(g) vieille

Test yourself 21 (a) un grand cheval noir (b) une petite sœur (c) les cheveux longs (d) chère Julie (e) un T-shirt cher (f) une jolie fille (g) des chaussures brunes (h) un professeur intelligent

Test yourself 22 (a) notre maison (b) votre tante (c) sa mère (d) ses chats (e) nos enfants (f) ta chambre (g) leur école (h) ma grand-mère

Test yourself 23 (a) à gauche de la boucherie (b) chez Simon (c) derrière le marché (d) pendant le match (e) en face de l'église (f) sous la table (g) sur la commode (h) à côté de la banque (i) avec mes amis (j) dans la salle de classe

Test yourself 24 (a) sans moi (b) pour lui (c) derrière toi (d) avant nous (e) avec elle (f) chez eux/chez elles

Chapter 3: Family, friends and pets

Test yourself 25

1 The following are examples of possible answers only.

(a) Salut!
(b) Enchanté(e) *or* Bonjour Monsieur, bonjour Madame.
(c) Je te présente ma sœur, Stephanie.
(d) Ça va?
(e) Rendez-vous à la piscine.
(f) Au revoir, à samedi.

2 (a) J'ai (b) J'ai (c) Je suis (d) J'ai (e) Je suis (f) Je suis (g) J'ai (h) Je suis (i) Je suis (j) J'ai

Chapter 4: House, home, daily routine and chores

Test yourself 26 1 (a) habite (b) est (c) met/débarrasse (d) brosse

Chapter 5: In town, travel and transport, food and drink

Test yourself 27 1 (a) 12 (b) 1 (c) 4, 14 (d) 8 (e) 6 (f) 5, 13 (g) 2 (h) 7 (i) 9 (j) 3 (k) 11, 15 (l) 10

2 The following are examples of possible answers only.

(a) à vélo
(b) en voiture
(c) en bateau
(d) en train
(e) en avion

Chapter 6: Free time

Test yourself 28

1 (a) 3
(b) 8
(c) 7
(d) 1
(e) 2
(f) 9
(g) 10
(h) 6
(i) 4
(j) 5

2 (a) aller
(b) écouter
(c) jouer
(d) faire
(e) bavarder

Chapter 7: Life and work at school

Test yourself 29

1 (a) 2
(b) 5
(c) 1
(d) 4
(e) 3

Chapter 8: Holidays, weather, time and dates

Test yourself 30

3

Positive		Negative	
génial	bon marché	bizarre	ennuyeux
excellent	intéressant	bruyant	trop court
extra	fantastique	nul	affreux
incroyable	chouette	désastreux	
super	tranquille	stressant	
bien	confortable	trop cher	
formidable	cool	trop long	

4 Activities often done on the beach:

(a) (b) (f)

Chapter 9: Health and fitness

Test yourself 31

1 (a) la bouche
(b) les jambes/les pieds
(c) les mains
(d) les yeux
(e) les jambes/les pieds

2 (a) (d) (f) (g) (j)

Appendix 1: Transcripts for the listening passages

Track 1

Exercise 3.7: Listen to Marc talking about himself and the members of his family and give at least two details for each one.

Salut! Moi, je m'appelle Marc et j'ai onze ans. J'ai les cheveux assez longs et bruns et les yeux bleus.

J'ai une grande famille: il y a mes deux parents et trois frères. Ma mère s'appelle Françoise et elle est petite et mince. Elle a les cheveux roux, courts et frisés.

Mon père s'appelle Philippe et il a quarante ans. Il est grand et un petit peu gros. Il a les yeux bleus et il est chauve.

Mes trois frères s'appellent Matthieu, Luc et Jean. Matthieu a quinze ans et il est très sportif. Il est musclé et bronzé et il adore jouer au rugby.

Luc a treize ans et il est très intelligent. Il a les cheveux bruns comme moi et il adore le rock.

Jean a cinq ans. Il a les cheveux blonds et courts, il est assez petit et très mignon. Il a des taches de rousseur.

Track 2

Exercise 3.8: Listen to the man talking about his family and pick the correct answer, as in the example.

Exemple: Je m'appelle Jean-Marc et j'ai cinquante ans.

(a) Il y a cinq personnes dans notre famille.

(b) J'ai deux fils et une fille.

(c) Ma femme a les cheveux longs et raides.

(d) Je suis professeur.

(e) Je quitte la maison à huit heures moins vingt-cinq.

Track 3

Exercise 4.4: Listen to the following passage and pick the phrases you hear from the list below.

Tous les jours je me réveille à sept heures et, dix minutes plus tard, je me douche. Je m'habille et puis je fais mon lit. À sept heures trente-cinq je descends pour prendre mon petit-déjeuner. Normalement, c'est Papa qui prépare le petit-déjeuner et moi je mets la table. Quand nous avons fini, Maman débarrasse la table et je donne à manger au chien.

Track 4

Exercise 5.4: Listen to these people and choose the place where they should go.

(a) Je viens d'écrire une lettre à ma tante mais je n'ai pas de timbres.

(b) Vous avez un plan de la ville, s'il vous plaît?

(c) Maman, il n'y a plus de jambon pour mon sandwich.

(d) Papa, j'ai très mal à la tête. Tu as des aspirines?

(e) Nous allons à la messe demain matin à dix heures.

Track 5

Exercise 5.5: Listen to the conversation and choose TRUE or FALSE for each sentence below, as in the example.

Le reporter:	Bonjour Anne. Tu as quel âge?
Anne:	J'ai treize ans.
Le reporter:	Est-ce que tu reçois de l'argent de poche?
Anne:	Oui mais je dois aider mes parents à la maison.
Le reporter:	Qu'est-ce que tu fais pour aider tes parents?
Anne:	Chaque matin je dois ranger ma chambre avant d'aller à l'école.
Le reporter:	Et qu'est-ce que tu fais le week-end?
Anne:	Je nettoie la maison avec Maman et je fais la vaisselle.
Le reporter:	Tu fais quelque chose avec ton père?
Anne:	Oui, mon père est handicapé. Nous aimons jouer aux échecs pendant que Maman fait les courses.
Le reporter:	Qu'est-ce que tu fais avec tes amis?
Anne:	S'il fait beau, je vais en ville avec mon amie Laura. Nous aimons acheter des vêtements et, quelquefois, nous allons au parc bavarder avec nos amis.

Track 6

Exercise 6.3: Listen to this telephone conversation and answer the questions below in English.

Marc:	Salut Anne. Tu veux aller au cinéma mercredi soir? Il y a un super film de science-fiction que j'ai envie de voir.
Anne:	Mercredi soir? Non, je ne peux pas. Je dois aller chez ma grand-mère car c'est son anniversaire. En plus, je déteste les films de science-fiction.
Marc:	La semaine prochaine alors? On pourrait aller au stade de rugby voir le match. Qu'en penses-tu?
Anne:	Bonne idée! On se retrouve où? Devant le stade?
Marc:	Je préfère en face de la bibliothèque parce qu'il y a moins de monde.
Anne:	Pas de problème. Et on se retrouve à quelle heure?
Marc:	Vers treize heures trente?
Anne:	Fantastique. Rendez-vous samedi prochain, treize heures trente en face de la bibliothèque. À la semaine prochaine.

Track 7

Exercise 7.5: Listen to Julie describe her school. For each sentence, choose the correct picture.

Exemple: Je me lève à sept heures.

(a) Je vais à l'école en car.

(b) J'arrive à l'école à huit heures dix.

(c) J'adore les ordinateurs.

(d) Mon sport préféré est le hockey mais mercredi après-midi, nous avons un match de tennis.

(e) Ce soir, mes parents vont chez ma grand-mère mais je dois rester chez moi faire mes devoirs.

Track 8

Exercise 7.6: Listen to the boy talking about his school and choose the correct answer, as in the example.

Exemple: Mon école se trouve à Bordeaux.

(a) C'est une école mixte.

(b) Il y a cent soixante-dix élèves.

(c) Ma matière préférée, c'est la physique.

(d) Le professeur de physique est petit avec les cheveux courts et frisés.

(e) Je ne suis pas sportif mais j'aime le théâtre.

Track 9

Exercise 7.7: Listen to this boy and choose a picture for each thing he says, as in the example.

Exemple: J'adore jouer de la trompette.

(a) Vite, Marc. Le court est libre en ce moment. Tu as les raquettes?

(b) Je voudrais être acteur.

(c) Tu aimes les poèmes?

(d) Je ne comprends pas les fractions.

(e) J'adore faire les expériences dans le labo.

Track 10

Exercise 8.12: Match each description you hear with the correct event below.

(a) C'est une fête d'origine chrétienne pour célébrer la résurrection de Jésus. Pour la plupart des Français c'est une fête non-religieuse où la famille se réunit pour manger un gigot d'agneau et des œufs en chocolat.

(b) C'est une fête qui marque le début de la nouvelle année. On rend visite à sa famille et à ses amis et souvent on envoie des cartes pour leur dire bonne année.

(c) C'est un jour qui symbolise la fin de la monarchie française et le début de la République. Le quatorze juillet se fête dans toute la France avec de la musique, de la danse, de la chanson et des feux d'artifice.

(d) C'est l'anniversaire de la fin du combat entre l'Allemagne et les Alliés après les quatre ans de la Première Guerre mondiale.